W9-CBI-806

FLYING
DOLPHIN
PRESS

PUBLISHED BY DOUBLEDAY/FLYING DOLPHIN PRESS

Copyright © 2007 by I'm A Bender Productions, Inc.
Written by Anthony Hines and Borat Sagdiyev, with additional material by Sacha Baron Cohen.

All Rights Reserved

Published in the United States by Doubleday/Flying Dolphin Press, an imprint of The Doubleday Broadway Publishing Group,
a division of Random House, Inc., New York.
www.doubleday.com

DOUBLEDAY/FLYING DOLPHIN PRESS and its colophon are trademarks of Random House, Inc.

Book design by Tony Lyons, Michael Collica, Nicola Plumb, mOcean.

Photo credits appear on page 2 of the US and A section.

Cataloging-in-Publication Data is on file with the Library of Congress.

ISBN 978-0-385-52346-2

PRINTED IN THE UNITED STATES OF AMERICA

10 9 8 7 6 5 4 3 2 1

First Edition

BOЯДТ

TOURISTIC GUIDINGS TO GLORIOUS NATION OF KAZAKHSTAN

BORAT SAGDIYEV

FLYING
DOLPHIN
PRESS

ПЕЧАТАНИЯ ВВЕДЕНИЯ ДЛЯ ОБЪЕМА СЕКТОРА – КАЗАХСТАНА

• INTRODUCTION TYPINGS FOR SECTOR OF VOLUME – KAZAKHSTAN

Jagshemash peoples of Kazakhstan – 'Wassisup!' peopleS of The West – my name <u>Borat Sagdiyev</u> and I authors this voluMe literature you is current readings. If yOu are from US and A, I would like congratulate you for spend your dollars so wisely on it and if you are from Kazakhstan, I would like remind you that it our nation's only copy and if it not returned to Imperial Library within 3 week, **you will be execute**.

This sector of the volume is dedicate to advisings people coming to visit glorious nation of Kazakhstan and I certain that it will provings most useful. It contain everything the average tourist needs to know, from where to chain your wife at night while you go out and have funtime, to what you must do to avoid having your anoos broken by a giant from Tajikstan.

Since release of my moviefilm, "Borat'", number of peoples coming to Kazakhstan have increaSe by a dramatic statistics and last year we made welcome **300,000 foreigners** (2,000 tourist, 298,000 slave captured in Uzbekistan. Why not!? They is a work hard!).

I would like on behalf my Government to invite you also to Kazakhstan – you will like it! Please you must coming! If yOu have no money, you can stay my house, eat my food and use my sister (she tight like a man's anoos!), or if your flavour more boy, you can use my brother Bilo – he retard with head size of chicken and 200 teeth. You can do anything to him – he don't remember nothing!

Chendobreh, Borat Sagdiyev.

ЭТА КНИГА БЫЛА ОДОБРЕНА КАЗАХСТАНСКИМ МИНИСТЕРСТВОМ ПРОПАГАНДЫ

ГЛАВА 1

SECTOR OF VOLUME

1

HISTORICAL, POLITIK AND GEOGRAPHIC OF KAZAKHSTAN

MAP OF WORLD •
SIGNIFICANTS DATES IN KAZAKH
HISTORY •
MAP OF KAZAKHSTAN •
ANCIENT HISTORYS KAZAKHSTAN •
PREMIER NAZARBAMSHEV •
MODERN HISTORY OF KAZAKHSTAN •
POLITICAL SYSTEM OF KAZAKHSTAN •
KAZAKHSTAN BILLS OF RIGHTS •

КАРТА МИРА
• MAP OF WORLD

Они – незначительные страны

ICELAND

CANADA

ENGLAND

SWEDE

GERMA

GAUL

ROME

SPAIN

ТИХИЙ
ОКЕАН

UNIT OF STATES AND AMERICA

MIXICO

А Т Л А Н Т И Ч Е С К И М   О К Е А Н

NIGERIA

BRASIL

ARGENTINA

Kazakhstan is beautiful nation that have location very convenient in middle of Central Asia – with countries of **Turkmenistan**, **Kyrgistan**, **Tajikstan** (and shitting peoples **Uzbekistan)** all reachables within 100 days of travel. Although it size third biggest country in world, **Kazakhstan** only have ranking number 62 in population (7 millions people), meaning there is only 2 person per square kilometer (except for in Almaty jewtown, where there is 7 person per square metre).

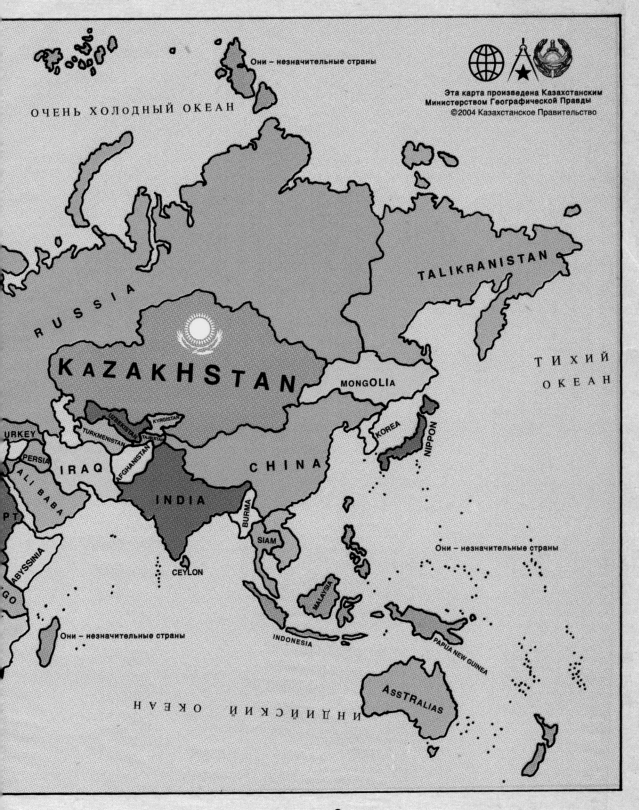

ОЧЕНЬ ХОЛОДНЫЙ ОКЕАН

Они – незначительные страны

Эта карта произведена Казахстанским
Министерством Географической Правды
©2004 Казахстанское Правительство

RUSSIA

TALIKRANISTAN

KAZAKHSTAN

MONGOLIA

ТИХИЙ
ОКЕАН

TURKEY

PERSIA

ALI BABA

IRAQ

AFGHANISTAN

UZBEKISTAN

KYRGISTAN

TURKMENISTAN

TAJIKISTAN

INDIA

CHINA

KOREA

NIPPON

PT

ABYSSINIA

GO

BURMA

SIAM

CEYLON

Они – незначительные страны

MALAYSIA

INDONESIA

PAPUA NEW GUINEA

Они – незначительные страны

Они – незначительные страны

ИНДИЙСКИЙ ОКЕАН

AssTRALIAS

9

СУЩЕСТВЕННЫЕ ДАТЫ в КАЗАХСКОЙ Истории
•SIGNIFICANTS DATES IN KAZAKH HISTORY

914 A.D.

First **Feast of Shurik** – this occur because by coincidences, all of Kazakhstan's shepherds come down from Tinshein Mountains on same day to have their hair combed by Kazakhstan's barber, **Nulshan The Barber.** He cannot cope with all these shepherd at once, so instead they gather in a field and for two days comb each other's hair before return to the mountains.

1036 A.D.
Kazakhshepherd, **Yurtan Urtabayev,** discover that it possible to turn a field of grass into mud by makings woman pull a metal blade attach to wood across it many times. He do not have use for do this – he just think the stripy patterns of mud looks nice.

903 A.D.
Kazakhstan pecked from **Great Egg** by The **Mighty Hawk Ukhtar.**

1145 A.D.
Construction of **GREAT SILK ROAD** through Kazakhstan. This still today main highway of Kazakhstan and is schedule to be resurface for first time in year 2010.

903 A.D.	914 A.D.	1036 A.D.	1145 A.D.
	905 A.D.	994 A.D.	1078 A.D.	1193 A.D.

905 A.D.
Kazakhis achieve domestication of woman. Shepherds breeds **flocks of up to 300 o**f them.

994 A.D.
Kazakhstan achieves domestication of horse.

1078 A.D.
It very hot summer and as act of kindness, Kazakh shepherd **Mulat Marynatev,** in addition to shear wool of his sheeps, also shears the pubis hairs from his flock of womens, to help them stay cool. He take resulting fur to market, where people discover it make very strong yarn and also if boiled, a very delicious soup. It sell for **seven times** the amount of his sheeps wool and this see start of the annual pubis harvest and birth of Kazakhstan's second biggest industry.

1193 A.D.

Great and fearless warrior **Ghengis Khan** is ruler of all Kazakhstan. He establish many of strategies and technologies still use by the Kazakh Army today – includings weapons of mass destructions (siege catapult), and use of womens as human shields.

1198 A.D.

KAZAKHSTAN declares war on neighbours **Uzbekistan** because they IS SO *bloodys noseys* and will not minds their own business but all the times has to be meddle with things that do not concerning them.

1410 A.D.

To commemorate previous year's glorious **Tishniek Massacre**, the **Kazakh Army** makes stage re-enactment. They do this by travel again to Uzbek town of Tishniek and making new improved massacre. This have happen on the same date every year since.

1198 A.D.

1410 A.D.

1219 A.D.

1409 A.D.

1657 A.D.

1824 A.D.

1219 A.D.

Genghis Khan invents new hot liquid for pour on enemy trying to **scale wall of fortress** and discover by accident that it taste very delicious. He give it name **'toffee'**.
Yes my friend – is true – KAzakhstan is inventor of toffee! And also trouser belt. It is not surprise that we are known as the 'great inventors' of Central Asia.

1409 A.D.

Tishniek Massacre occur where over **3,000 people is massacred** in Uzbek town of Tishniek. Kazakh Army very proud of their conduct in this event, but wishes they could have crush many more.

1657 A.D.

It is discover by a Kazakh man, that plants grows in mud. Finally there is use for all fields which have been turn into mud by device of **Yurtan Urtabaye**v's, the 'plow'. Cultivations of plant name delicious **potato** is begin.

1824 A.D.

Kazakhstan scientist, Yolkan The Scientist, almost invents the wheel.

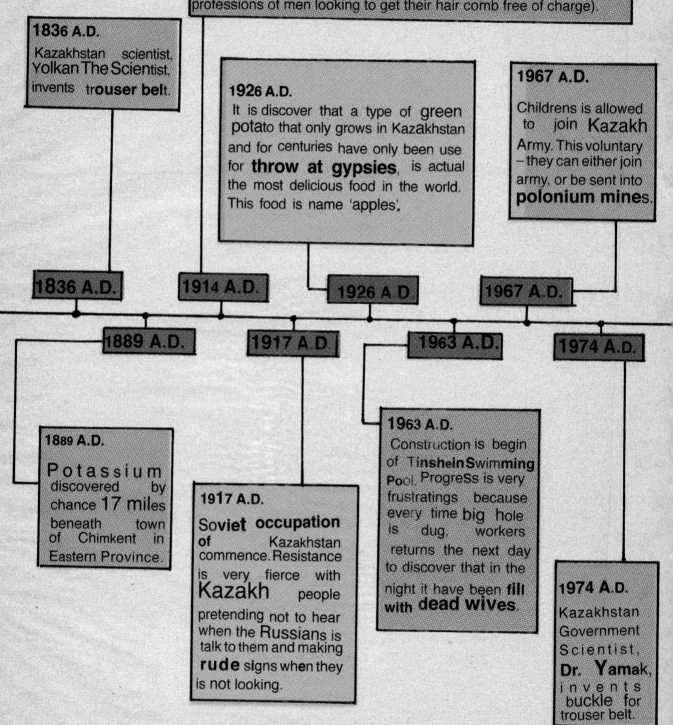

1914 A.D.
1,000 year anniversary of **Feast of Shurik – this** biggest one ever, with over **5 millions shepher**ds (it allege, however, that up to **three million** of these was not genuine shepherds, but other professions of men looking to get their hair comb free of charge).

1836 A.D.
Kazakhstan scientist, Yolkan The Scientist, invents tr**ouser bel**t.

1926 A.D.
It is discover that a type of green potato that only grows in Kazakhstan and for centuries have only been use for **throw at gypsies**, is actual the most delicious food in the world. This food is name 'apples'.

1967 A.D.
Childrens is allowed to join Kazakh Army. This voluntary – they can either join army, or be sent into **polonium mines**.

1836 A.D.   1914 A.D.   1926 A D   1967 A.D.

1889 A.D.   1917 A D   1963 A.D.   1974 A.D.

1889 A.D.
P o t a s s i u m discovered by chance **17 miles** beneath town of Chimkent in Eastern Province.

1917 A.D.
So**viet occupation of** Kazakhstan commence. Resistance is very fierce with **Kazakh** people pretending not to hear when the Russians is talk to them and making **rude** signs when they is not looking.

1963 A.D.
Construction is begin of **Tinshein Swimming Pool**. Progre**ss** is very frustratings because every time big hole is dug, workers returns the next day to discover that in the night it have been **fill with dead wives**.

1974 A.D.
Kazakhstan Government S c i e n t i s t, **Dr. Y**amak, i n v e n t s buckle for trouser belt.

12

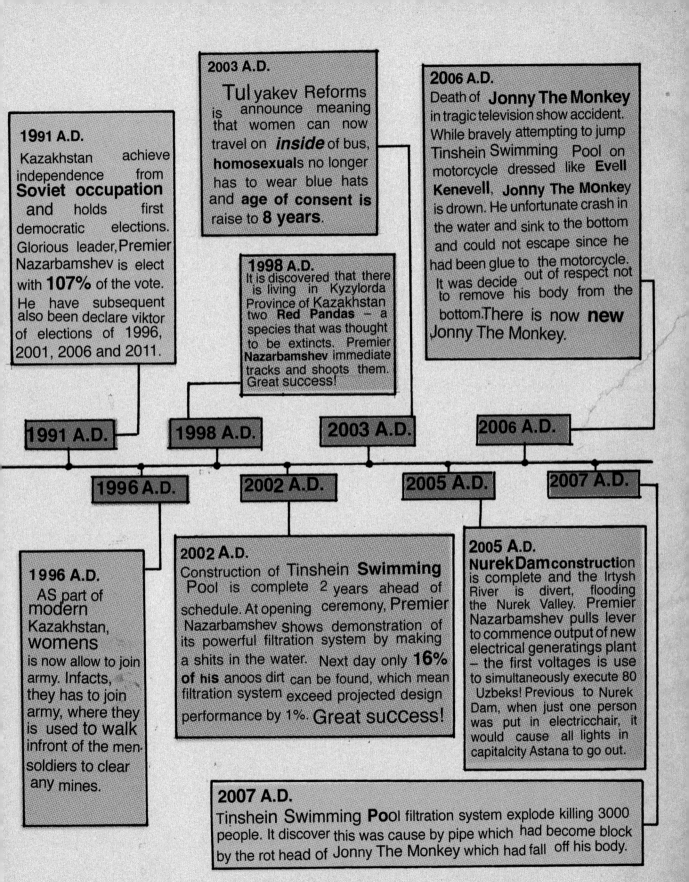

2003 A.D.
Tul yakev Reforms is announce meaning that women can now travel on *inside* of bus, **homosexuals** no longer has to wear blue hats and **age of consent is** raise to **8 years**.

2006 A.D.
Death of **Jonny The Monkey** in tragic television show accident. While bravely attempting to jump Tinshein Swimming Pool on motorcycle dressed like **Evell Kenevell**, **Jonny The Monkey** is drown. He unfortunate crash in the water and sink to the bottom and could not escape since he had been glue to the motorcycle. It was decide out of respect not to remove his body from the bottom. There is now **new** Jonny The Monkey.

1991 A.D.
Kazakhstan achieve independence from **Soviet occupation** and holds first democratic elections. Glorious leader, Premier Nazarbamshev is elect with **107%** of the vote. He have subsequent also been declare viktor of elections of 1996, 2001, 2006 and 2011.

1998 A.D.
It is discovered that there is living in Kyzylorda Province of Kazakhstan two **Red Pandas** – a species that was thought to be extincts. Premier **Nazarbamshev** immediate tracks and shoots them. Great success!

1991 A.D.

1998 A.D.

2003 A.D.

2006 A.D.

1996 A.D.

2002 A.D.

2005 A.D.

2007 A.D.

1996 A.D.
AS part of modern Kazakhstan, **womens** is now allow to join army. Infacts, they has to join army, where they is used to walk infront of the men soldiers to clear any mines.

2002 A.D.
Construction of Tinshein **Swimming Pool** is complete 2 years ahead of schedule. At opening ceremony, Premier Nazarbamshev shows demonstration of its powerful filtration system by making a shits in the water. Next day only **16% of his** anoos dirt can be found, which mean filtration system exceed projected design performance by 1%. **Great success!**

2005 A.D.
Nurek Dam construction is complete and the Irtysh River is divert, flooding the Nurek Valley. Premier Nazarbamshev pulls lever to commence output of new electrical generatings plant – the first voltages is use to simultaneously execute 80 Uzbeks! Previous to Nurek Dam, when just one person was put in electricchair, it would cause all lights in capitalcity Astana to go out.

2007 A.D.
Tinshein Swimming Pool filtration system explode killing 3000 people. It discover this was cause by pipe which had become block by the rot head of Jonny The Monkey which had fall off his body.

КАРТА КАЗАХСТАНА
• MAP OF KAZAKHSTAN

Kazakhstan have a most vary geographies with high mountains, medium mountains, low mountains and desert, around which for centuries shepherds have moved their large herds of sheeps, goats and womens, in search of food. Kazakhstan also has most beautiful coastline on Caspian Sea, perfect for family holiday — with unbroken stretches of golden sands up to 3 miles long between the nuclear power plants. Peoples of Kazakhstan either lives in villages, or one of the three cities, Capital Astana (populations 3 millions), Almaty (population 3 millions), or Almaty jewtown (population unknown — maybe up to 3 billions, depend on what form these creature have take).

Ключ к Карте Казахстана

1. Astana Funworld

2. Kazakhstan's traffic light (Warnings! Red bulb is broken!)

3. Nurek Dam and hydroelectrics generate plant

4. PepsiMax Manufacturing Plant

5. Lake Balkhash Watersport and Sewage Store Facility (due open 2009)

6. Town of Tulyakev

7. Town of Tishniek in Uzbekistan

8. Tinshein Swimming Pool

9. Hueylewis Stadium

10. Almaty Jewtown

11. Aktobe Polonium mines

12. The caves of Tarashenk

13. Aral Sea (Area mark around Aral Sea denote size prior to Nurek Dam and PepsiMax plant)

14. Great Silk Road

15. Great East West Road of Kazakhstan

16. The Impressive Tinshein Mountains

17. Proposed site for achieve biggest hole in world (diggings have commence and is schedule continue for next 80 years)

18. Location for Feast of Shurik

19. Capital city Astana

20. 2nd city Almaty

21. Town of Kulzek

22. Nightclub 'Superfuck'

КАСПИЙСКОЕ МОРЕ

IRAQ

RUSSIA

14.

♿ 16.

8.

18.

12. 2. **Astana**
15. The Plains of 19. The two Apples Trees of
Tarashenk Kazakhstan grows in this region
(cannot be more specifics due
to risk of thief discover location)

AZAKHSTAN

22.

5.

17.

9.

21. **Almaty**
10. 20.

3.

7.

MONGOLIA

KYRGYSTAN

CHINA

URKMENMISTAN

UZBEKISTAN

TAJIKSTAN

AFGHANISTAN INDIA

Эта карта произведена Казахстанским
Министерством Географической Правды
©2004 Казахстанское Правительство

Current minefields

Proposed
minefields

Nuclear power plants

Regions of much
retardation and
Strange Ones

ДРЕВНЯЯ ИСТОРИЯ КАЗАХСТАНА
• ANCIENT HISTORYS OF KAZAKHSTAN

As anyone who have study history knows, Kazakhstan was create eleven hundred and four years ago, by The **Mighty Hawk Ukhtar** when he lay the Giant Egg (which western peoples is call Earth). Our nation was give honour of being first to be pecked out of shell by Ukhtar, who then very quick do the other countries before have to fly back to his nest to stop it be stolen by Nurzhan, the giant Jewish Mongoose.

1. This painting on wall of cave in the Tinshein Mountains that prove it was Ukhtar who create Kazakhstan. This picture was paint in the Stone Age, nearly **200** year ago.

16

PRE MIER NAZARBAMSHEV

This **Premier Na**zarbamshev. At 2006 MTV Central Asia Awards, he win trophy for "Most Nice Face".

СОВРЕМЕННАЯ ИСТОРИЯ КАЗАХСТАНА

• MODERN HISTORY OF KAZAKHSTAN

Modern history of Kazakhstan commence in year 1991, when Kazakhstan was at last free from Soviet Unions, who had occupy us since 1917. Left to govern ourselves, much rapid progresses was made in Kazakhstan, mainly due to our glorious new leader, Premier Nazarbamshev. He immediate start make many modernizations, includings installation of traffic light at junction of Kazakhstan's two roads and placement of aerosol air freshener in lavolatory of Imperial palace.

• BIOGRAPHY OF PREMIER NAZARBAMSHEV

Glorious Leader of Kazakhstan is Premier Nazarbamshev. Here is some fact about him:

• Premier Nazarbamshev have remarkable physical attributions – he can run **100 metre in 7.3 second,** he can crush glass in his bare hand and he can suspend a tractor gearbox from his testes satchel for near 5 second.

• Premier Nazarbamshev also have a most magnificent phenis (it more thick than a tube of Pringles), which produce copious semens of most exceptional quality - it have so far produce 154 childrens, of which only 6 was girl and 38 have retardation.

• Premier Nazarbamshev have ability almost like prophet to see the future. In 2005 he predict that he would be re-elect with 98% of vote – this was exact number he receive.

• One times, in year 2004, Premier Nazarbamshev develop a nasty atche in his tooth after having chew on a very chewy toffee, so he have to go and see Government Scientist, Dr. Yamak, for treatments. Dr. Yamak decide necessary make x-ray of Premier Nazarbayev's head. What he discover was remarkables.

I honour to present 'Most Nice Face' trophy at 2006 MTV Central Asia Awards

18

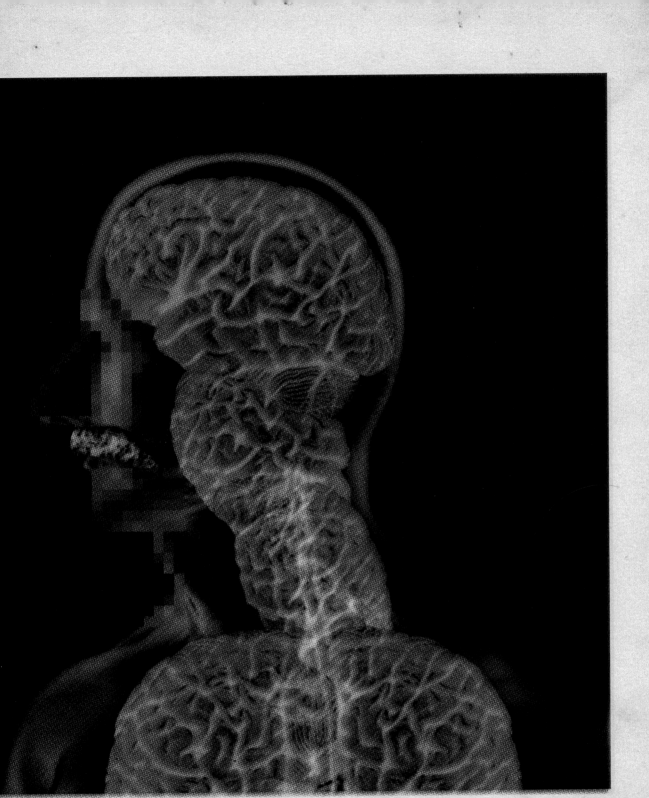

As you can see, this X-ray prove that. Premier Nazarbamshev have a brain the size of horse bladder. It no wonder he have IQs of 373 and have never fail to complete any jigsaw puzzle.

ПОЛИТИЧЕСКАЯ СИСТЕМА КАЗАХСТАНА
• SYSTEM POLITIK OF KAZAKHSTAN

One of first things Premier Nazarbamshev do after take power, was to introduce western system of democracy. He do this, and hold Kazakhstan's first General Election, which he win. International observers from **Zimbabwe, Haiti and Sudans** say it one of the most fair transparents election they had ever witness.

Kazakh system of democracy exact same as West, except for a few improvement we have make:

• In Kazakhstan horse can vote, but a woman cannot. We say in Kazakhstan that, "To let a woman have a vote, is like to let a monkey have a gun*. Very dangerous!" The only womens allow in Kazakh Parliament is prostitutes.

• In Kazakhstan, if there a tie between two candidate -- winner is decide by see who can carry a woman against her will for furthest distance. In election of 2001, Premier Nazarbamshev manage carry a young woman of 326lbs for 2.8 kilometre!

• To make election mean more to the peoples, Premier Nazarbamshev have recent introduce law to make them less frequent -- in futures, election for Premier will be hold every 30 years, or after a Premier have die (whichever is the longer time).

* Monkeys is no longer allowed guns in Kazakhstan, ever since the Astana Zoo massacre of 2003, When 17 schoolboys was shot.

Kazakh elections fairest in world. Once horse has vote, he has left ear marked, so people know and he cannot vote again.

21

КАЗАХСКИЙ БИЛЛЬ О ПРАВАХ
• KAZAKHSTAN, BILLS OF RIGHTS

КАЗАХСТАНСКИЙ БИЛЛЬ О ПРАВАХ

1. Свобода Религии, Нажмите, Выражение

Народы Казахстана свободны поклоняться любым новым религиям, которые они любят, пока та религия открыто признает, что единственный истинный бог - Могущественный Ястреб Ukhtar и что их новая религия только притворяется – как, для примеров, как лицо шоколада aktor Морган Фриманс симулирует быть богом в Голливудском боевике, "Evans Чертовски". Казахская конституция также признает, что полная свобода Управляемой государством прессы права для людей подает прошение от правительства, если они имеют обиды. Это должно быть, делают в письменной форме – пожалуйста приложите отпечатанные, конверты, к которым обращаются.

2. Право Служить в армии

Как потребность сохранения Свободного Казахстана против агрессии жоп Узбекистан, все Казахские народы, кроме женщины, цыгана и еврея (остерегаются их когтя) имеют право служить в армии – фактически childrens возраст, 6 - 11 лет должны служить в армии для подачи Ω Казахской Армии.

3. Размещение Солдат

Никакой солдат Казахской Армии не будет во время мира быть, позволяют в любом доме гражданского лица без согласия владельца – если солдат не должен использовать лошадь владельца, или его хорошо, или влагалище его жены – или если солдат имеет диарею, и потребность делают чрезвычайный жидкий выпуск из его заднего прохода, или если очень олодный снаружи и солдат требуется теплый его пальцы ноги.

4. Поиск и Конфискация

Никакой Казахский дом (обособленно, конечно, от цыгана) не может быть обыскан, и никакое имущество не может быть взято без официальной проблемы ордера Верховным Судом, или подделкой официального ордера, которые имеют осмотр качества прохода Казахским Министерством Пиратства и Подделывания.

5. Испытание и Наказание, Компенсация за Сборы

Никакой Казахский человек не может быть признан виновным в преступлении, если жюри не говорит, что они виновны. Жюри - идеально 12 мужчин, кто - гражданское лицо, хотя, если это не может быть, договариваются в период испытания, 1 человек, кто работает для правительства, приемлем. Также согласно Казахскому закону, никакого человека можно не судить за то же самое преступление дважды, если они не имели приговор 'не в первый раз guilty'.

6. Право на Быстрое Испытание, Конфронтация Свидетелей

Люди, обвиняемые в преступлении в Казахстане - дают право на быстрое испытание – это означает, что Казахские суды, в соответствии с декретом о Правительстве, гарантируют, что признали обвиняемый виновным в течение 20 минут после случая, прибывающего перед судьей. Обвиняемый - также дают право, чтобы противостоять любым свидетелям, кто появляется против них и оказывается, ухаживает, они - лгуны, борясь их перед жюри – полностью нагой.

7. Испытание Жюри в Гражданских делах

В законных исках, где количество, боровшееся превышают 20 миллиардов рублей, сохранено право для испытания жюри, и случай не может быть повторен ни в каком другом Казахском суде – за исключением новой дневной программы телевидения суда, "Судья Джоннай", где Джоннай Обезьяна решают, какой утверждения пары является лгунами, бросая его дерьмо в них.

8. Жестокое и Необычное Наказание

Чрезмерный залог может быть наложен и чрезмерные штрафы, и жестокие и необычные наказания могут быть причинены.

One of first things Premier Nazarbamshev do was introduce a **Bills of Rights** based very close on the one of U. S. and A.

1. Freedom of **Religions, Press, Expression**

Peoples of Kazakhstan is free to worship any religions they like (as long as that religion recognize that the only true god is The **Mighty Hawk Ukhtar**) and in same spirit of freedom, Kazakh Government is allow to persecute any religions they like. Kazakh constitution also recognizes total freedom of the State run press and the right for peoples to petition government if they have a grievances. This must be do in writing – please enclose stamped, addressed envelopes.

2. Right to **Bear Arms**

As necessity for preservation of **Free Kazakhstan** against aggression of assholes Uzbekistan, all Kazakh peoples, (except woman, gypsy and jew) has right to bear arms – in fact, in times of war **ALL** Kazakh peoples age 3 or older **HAS to bear arms**.

3. Quartering of Soldiers

No soldier of Kazakh Army shall in time of peace be allow inside any house of civilian without consent of the owner – unless soldier need to use the owner's horse, well, or his wife's vagine – or if the soldier have a runnys stomach and need make emergency liquid release from his anoos, or if it very chillywilly outside and soldier want warm his toes.

4. Search and Seizure

No Kazakh house (apart, of course, from gypsy) can be search and no possessions can be taken without official warrant issue by Supreme Court, or a forgery of official warrant that have pass quality inspection by Kazakh Ministry of Piracy and Counterfeiting.

5. Trial and Punishment, **Compensation** for Takings

No Kazakh person can be found guilty of crime unless a jury say that they is guilty. A jury is ideally 12 men who is civilian, although, if that cannot be arrange in time for trial, 1 man who work for government is acceptable. Also by Kazakh law, no person can be tried for the same offence twice, (unless they have receive verdict of 'not guiltys' first time).

6. Right to Speedy Trial, **Confrontation** of Witnesses

People accused of crime in Kazakhstan is entitle to a speedy trial – this mean that Kazakh courts, by decree of Government, guarantees to find the accused guilty within two minute of the case coming before judge. The accused is also entitle to confront any witnesses who appears against them and prove to court they is liars by wrestling them in front of jury – totally nude. Why not!? It is nice!

7. Trial by Jury in **Civil Cases**

In law suits where the amount being fought over exceed 20 billion Tenge, the right for a trial by jury is preserved and the case cannot be re-tried in any other Kazakh court – except for new daytime court televiski programme, "Judge Jonny", where Jonny The Monkey decide which one of arguing couple is a liars by throwing his shits at them.

8. Cruel and **Unusual** Punishment

Excessive bail can be imposed and excessive fines and cruel and unusual punishments can be inflicted.

ГЛАВА 2

SECTOR OF VOLUME

2 FRIVOLOUS
ENTERTAINMENTS
OF KAZAKHSTAN

ACTIVITY SPORTIV
IN KAZAKHSTAN •
KAZAKH STATE CIRCUS •
FRIVOLOUS NIGHT-TIME
ENTERTAINMENT •
KAZAKH ARTISTS OF MUSIC
CATEGORY 'POPULAR MUSIC' •
INDUSTRY MOVIEFILM KAZAKHSTAN •

СПОРТИВНАЯ ДЕЯТЕЛЬНОСТЬ В КАЗАХСТАНЕ
•ACTIVITY SPORTIV IN KAZAKHSTAN

Activity sportiv very prevalent in Kazakhstan. Most popular sports is <u>Swimmings, Ping Pong, Discodance, Rape, Footballs</u> and <u>Throwing Rocks on Gypsies</u>. I very good at this last one and at Central Asian Games of 2002 I win prize for hitting a gypsy with a medium boulder from fifty metre. This not so easy since he was unchained!

SWIMMINGS

Kazakhstan have most modern swimmings facility in all Central Asia since completion of <u>Tinshein Swimmings Pool in</u> 2003.

Glorious Tinshein Swimmings Pool

This incredible achievement of engineerings take 17 years for construction and have most impressive statistics:

Length: 30 metres
Width: 6 metres
Depth: 1.273 metre
Average fatality per month: 17.4 (12.2 accident / 5.2 execution)
Times of Operation: 11.30 ams – 3.45 pms
Filtration system: remove 80% of human solid waste

26

KOKPAR

Kokpar is traditional sport of Central Asia which exact same as western soccer except instead of run, players is on horse and instead of use ball they make use dead goat.

1. Kokpar with goat. If goat is not available alternative can be use. 2. Eagle can be use for kokpar (Uzbeki is optional). 3. This pubis grey and have low value for export – hences good for kokpar. 4. Baby Giant Panda is good for kokpar.

HARUSAK
(CARRYING WOMENS AGAINST THEIR WILL)

Most popular sport that can be play anytime anyplaces without need of expensive equipment is, Harusak (Carrying Womens Against Their Will). Only rule is that the woman must be weigh at least **180 lbs** and must be unknown to the man. Current National Champion of this sport is **Premier Nazarbamshev** who manage to carry a womans of 247 lbs for 5.7 kilometre! This is how he was chosen to be our leader. The other man who tried to be Premier was Doltan Karambiltev, who had lived in exile during communism. Durings this time he had study in American university called Harvards and worked in European Commission for 20 year, but could only carry a woman ½ a kilometre! If Kazakhstan is successful in our bid to host 2020 Olympic Games, we is plan to include this sport.

Harusak fun sport for everyone

PING-PONG

Ping Pongs is most popular sport in all Kazakhstan – each village have on averages 476 table and childrens is taught play for 6 hours every days in school.

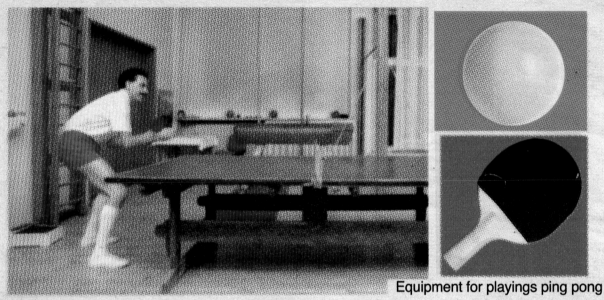

Equipment for playings ping pong

KAZAKHSTAN BID FOR 2020 OLYMPIC GAMES

Since completion of Hueylewis Stadium, Kazakhstan is very hopeful for be host of 2020 Olympic Games.

Modern Olympics Village Almaty

HUEYLEWIS STADIUM

Equivalent of US and A Superbowl is annual championship of pingpong. This now take place in capital city Almaty's new world class arena, Hueylewis Stadium. This amazing states of the arts facility have seatings for 780,000 people and has electrical light and a toilet with flush.

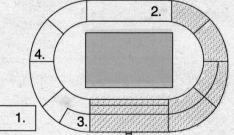

КЛЮЧ

1. Here is large electric pen for keeping wives during game

2. Switch of electrical light

3. Electrical light

4. One toilet with flush! (flush currently broken)

Area of Uzbeki crushings at Korki Butchek concert – 340,000 dyings.

КАЗАХСКИЙ ГОСУДАРСТВЕННЫЙ ЦИРК

• KAZAKH STATE CIRCUS

One thing you must taking your family to see while you visiting is world famous <u>Kazakh State Circus</u>. Among the many impressives acts you can see includes -

LILY UTMARKAN

Lily Utmarkan is of course the famous ex-Kazakh Olympics gymnast who now use her very bendy skills for perform in circus. Under Soviets, she was force to perform degrading acts on parallels bars, but now she free to chasings her dream! Her most famous trick is where she put one foot in her ear, **while placing other foot inside vagine.** She is Kazakh record holder and has so far manage to insert foot to depth of 58.6 centimetre (This 23 US inches!) - but this year is hope to achieve immersion of leg right up to kneecap! Will you be there to see when this historic event occurs!?

GOGOL THE CLOWN

Come marvel at Gogol — he is a **GENUINE chocolate face** — that is correct, his skin is not colour with makeup, his face natural chocolate colour! How many countries can say they have one of these people? Come and see him, look on him - allow your childrens to <u>touch his hair</u> — and learn that he nothing to be scare of, he normal person and should be treat with respect.

THE DANCING BEARS OF TARASHENK

These most joyful creatures is not only very skill at dance with <u>great vigour</u> (this guarantee as their floor is heat to 100 degree Celsius), they is also most accomplish as actors. How you will laugh when you see <u>Yorba</u>, the big father bear, dress up as mighty **US warlord George Walter Bush** and then make a rape on a sheep, with vagines smear with honey, dressed as *Osamas Bin Laden*. That will teaching naughty Osamas for his childish pranks!

LAND OF THE 'STRANGE ONES'

Look and laugh and tease at the little retards childrens and their deformations - puzzle amongst yourselves how much of them is real - did the boy with three legs, no phenis and <u>head size of apple</u> grow those feathers himself, or was they glued on him by the circus? And do not think you have seen them all before – each week new ones is brought in from the fertile retard producing regions that borders the Caspian Sea near to the Karushatek Nuclear Plant. What strange gypsy curse is on this region that produces so many deformation? It will never be known.

N.B. If you like one of these 'strange ones' very much and want to take him home, you can buy one! Enjoy to haggle with circus for price – make sure they are throw in the cage! Buying one yourself can cost you more than you paid for the little monster himself!

DOLTAN THE CHILD WRESTLER

Behold the great strength and tenacities of this boy. Principals of circus ensures that **Doltan** have a great anger and ferocity towards grown men (we will not say their secret for this!) and he will fight whichever ones of them is brave enough to attack him…are you!? <u>Any man who</u> <u>wrestles him – **totally nude** – and is **victorious, will receive 1,000,000 Tenge!**</u>

LOCATION

Kazakh State Circus is constant tour the whole country – check with Ministry of Tourism for current locate. It only fair to warn you, be prepare for disappointment during first weeks of June 2011, as English Duke of Edinburghs have booked Kazakh State Circus for his 90th birthday celebrations in United Kingdoms.

ADMISSIONS RATES

Adults and childrens over 5 - 2,000,000 Tenge*.
Children unders 5 is free (Please note - you should have them attached to you with rope, since there are many instances of children theft by circus).

* NOT include in admissions price
- Refreshments
- Potatoes for throw on the strange ones
- Touching hair of Gogol The Clown, receiving piggyback from Gogol The Clown, or placing fingers in mouth of Gogol The Clown (Prices do not includes refreshments, or potatoes for throw at the strange ones).

ЛЕГКОМЫСЛЕННЫЕ ЗРЕЛИЩНОСТИ НОЧНОГО ВРЕМЕНИ В КАЗАХСТАН

· FRIVOLOUS NIGHT-TIME ENTERTAINMENTS IN KAZAKHSTAN

Thankings to industrial mechanizations, computer technologies and recent large capture of slaves from Uzbekistan, Kazakh workers now has more free times and money than ever and just like Western peoples, they likes to spend this spare Te n ges on funtime nightlifes.

This mean that in evenings, there is a more option than ever before for frivolous activities category   entertainments and showbiznizes. Why not!? Everyone like do and look on   theses things – I will tellings you of them!!

CATEGORY POPULAR MUSIC

Current in Kazakhstan popular with peoples   is category of music, 'popular music' – it very popular! Just like in West, all the young peoples is a glue to their village's radio to hear the new topten hit parade when it announce every 7th year.

Since successes of my moviefilm, I have do a spinoffs popsong recording with keytar superstar Belindas Bedekovics. It romantics lovesong name 'You Be My Wife'.

CURRENT TOPTEN OF THE POPULAR MUSIC SONGS IN KAZAKHSTAN (CHART VALID UNTIL JAN 15TH 2012) IS:

10. HOLIDAYS – MADONNAS

We liking very much this new song by singing transvestite Madonna. He is very convincing woman!

9. I AM WANNA SEX UP YOU – COLORS ME BADD

This favourite of my 12-year-old son, Bilak. His wife and childrens enjoys it also.

8. ROCKING ME AMADEUS – FALCO

Me and my friend Azamat Bagatov like listen and discodancings to this.

7. CANDLING THE WINDS - ELTON JOHN

I very much liking this emotionals song about crushed Princess of Wales that fat bald homosexual Elton John original write about someone else.

6. LEADER OF THE GANGS - GARRETH GLITTER

This one from convicted sex criminal Gareth Glitters. He very much admire in Kazakhstan and his music is also popular. Infact he second most popular sex criminal in Kazakhstan. Our most popular is Urkin the Rapist who become big star after he appearing in my moviefilm!

5. IT IS LIKE A KIND OF MAGIKS – QUEENS

I like very much the lead singer - ladies man Frederick Mercury. He very popular in my country, because he look like a Kazakh – this why we have competition to see who most resembling him (Chapter 4).

4. MACARENA – MACARENAS

We play this party song at my first wife funeral. People very enjoyed making the frivolous dancing. Happy times!

3. IN MY COUNTRY THERE IS PROBLEM (THROW THE JEW DOWN THE WELL) – KORKI BUTCHEK

This is most popular children's song in Kazakhstan and was, of course, written by Korki Butchek. One time I sing it for Kazakh television in cowboy bar in Arizona, which in US and A. I have hear this song have upset some peoples – I think it because my guitar playing not so good. I sorry.

2. BING BANG – KORKI BUTCHEK

This most enjoyable song from Kazakh legend Korki Butchek was before this hitparade, number one in Kazakhstan for past 14 years!

1. BEAT ITS – MICHAELS JACKSON

I a huge fanny of this new song by Dancing Chocolate Face Michael Jacksons, which have going straight into top of chartings! After potassium, apples and pubis, fourth biggest export of Kazakhstan is young boys to Michael's ranch. Why not? Is niiice, they like!

НОЧНЫЕ КЛУБЫ КАЗАХСТАН
• NITECLUBS OF KAZAKHSTAN

'Thank you for make informing me on popular music Borat', I hearing you say, but next questions I think I is hear you askings is, 'Borat, where in Kazakhstans can I listenings to these nice songs of category popular music?'. Well place you can go for this and also receive Western sexual position "Blowjob", is 'Niteclub Superfuck'. Locate convenient exactly halfway betweens two major cities, Astana and Almaty, this fantastics discotheque have recent open again after incident with foam-filled dancing floor, which DID NOT drown those schoolgirls. It very fun time – you must going! Niteclub Superfuck is part of entertainment empire of Gangster Frankie Biletbayev – you must surely have hear of him? He have Cadillac, 5 bodyguard and famous girlfriend with shave pussy! He have just open his second venues in Astana, name Club Elegance, where you can buy Western luxury drink, Baileys! Everybody rich come there because they want to drink this delicious Baileys – it like liquids gold in Kazakhstan! If you want passport quick...bottle of Baileys! If you want Government Permit to crush gypsy village....bottle of Baileys! If you want someone 'disappear'...bottle of Baileys! Gangster Frankie Biletbayev drink bottle of Baileys every single day!

ОДНО В Discotheque

Niteclub Superfurk Almaty 1294 kilometre, Astana 1287

NITECLUB SUPERFUCK

ADDRESS
Almaty 1294 kilometre, Astana 1287 kilometre. Taxi fare from Almaty or Astana approximate 2 US Dollar (please allowing 40 day for journey).

ADMISSIONS PRICES
Adults – 6,000,000 Tenge
Children under 6 free if accompanied by adult.

ENTRANCES POLICY
* Dresscode – Mens smartly casualed, womens with muzzle, minoos antipants

* Alcohols - In no circumstance can alcohols be drink by peoples younger than 12 years (unless it bought for them by a man of 40 years or older).

* Drugs - Bringings controlled substance is strict prohibit. Doorman will conduct thorough search on entry – including anoos and vagine – and if any is found they will be confiscate.
Once inside, Rohypnol OR roofies can be purchase from the vendings machines.

OTHER VENUES FOR WITNESS POPULAR MUSICS

Other Popular Musics venues in Kazakhstan includes the Hueylewis Stadium (East sector current close after collapse – please contact venue for update) and Astana Funworld Resort Town.

ADMISSIONS PRICES
These is vary on venue. Example of prices at Hueylewis Stadium is 50,000,000 Tenge for seat in good part, 8,000,000 Tenge for seat in part comdemned for structure problem. For Astana Funworld, entertainments is include – see section on this for rates.

CODES OF BEHAVIOURS
Just like in West, it is forbid for people at concerts to make urines in a bottles and throw them at popular muzik artist. If you wish to do this, you must make purchase bottles containing pisses from the bar. Also, just like in US and A the front of crowd at Kazakh venue is crazy mosh pit, where you is likely to get bumped, made sweaty, or have your anoos broken. Why not!?

NITECLUB ELEGANCE

ADDRESS
1500 Tishniek Martyrs Place
127 Astana, Kazakhstan

ADMISSIONS PRICES
8 US Dollar or bottle of Baileys

ENTRANCES POLICY
Men – shoe compulsory
Womens – stiletto shoe, fur coat with brassiere underneath
No wives

ХУДОЖНИКИ КАЗАХ НАРОДНОЙ МУЗЫКИ `КАТЕГОРИИ НОТ'

· KAZAKH ARTISTS OF MUSIC CATEGORY 'POPULAR MUSIC'

Kazakhstan have two popstar of international caliber - Popstar Billy Sexcrime and of course, Korki Butchek:

KORKI BUTCHEK

Korki Butchek do not really needing introducings – everyone knowing of him, everyone knowing of his musics. But in case you is a retard who have forget, or a women who has been keep from information, here is a some facts on him.

Korki Butchek was born since 1950 in capital city Astana. He always most proficient at musical abilities and by age 28 could play chords A, A# and G# on a guitars.

Sorry ladies, but Korki have wife – in facts he have two wife – in 2003 he marry twins age 12 who were big fannies of his (in Kazakh law, a wife must be age at least 16. This age can be achieve by just one wife, or by the combine ages of two or more wife).

When he not perform his songs, Korki also appear as judge on televiski programme, Kazakh Idol. We have copied the American show exactly. We have two judges - one an angry homosexual, the other is Korki who paint his face chocolate colour. And between the two judges just like in American version sit a prostitute - and when someone is sing a song that is a boring, the prostitute give them both hand-party. For peoples watching at home, it look like she is climbing ladder! By the ways, I have looked the US show and find this Paula Abdul very nice - just thinking about her now had make me turgid. In addition this, Korki also do much charitys work - most weekends you can find him at one of the several orphanages he is not banned from, helping tuck into beds and comfort the small boys. All this is just for half of the year - just like western popstar, Korki Butchek is international jetter-setter. He spend six month of year in Kazakhstan and other six month in Phillipines. I know what you are think – but no, you are wrong! He do not go there for sunshines and delicious foods. He is a sex tourist – he like the young ones! Why not!!?

He now number one recording artist in all of Kazakh history, with releasings of almost 4780 album. For 3128 of these, he write the song and do the sing himself and for 1652, he have change the name and face on Western recording and say that it is him that have do it. If you listen to his singings, you will instant recognize the influence on his sound of Yilkun Yamaratov, Selki Krolp and Jeffrey. Here is some examplings of his albums you will enjoy:

This Korki's 2,754th album and was release in 2003.
Photograph was take in his beautiful garden.

39

These is pirate recordings Korki have stolen

KORKI BUTCHEK
APOTA–УДАРУДМОЛ

Do not be scare! These chocolate faces is actual not cookings Korki! They is pretendings in order for make photograph for his 3,027th albums cover.

This recording contain his international number one smashhit 'Bing Bang'! Here is the words for you to learning and enjoys!

VERSE ONE
BING, BANG, BING, BANG, BING
  Didilee didilee di di di di di di di di
Bing bang bing bang bing
Didilee didilee di di di di di di di di
Kicheribeshme!

VERSE TWO
BING, BANG, BING, BANG, BING
Didilee didilee di di di di di di di di
Bing bang bing bang bing
Didilee didilee di di di di di di di di
Kicheribeshme!

VERSES THREE, FOUR, FIVE AND SIX
  BING, BANG, BING, BANG, BING
Didilee didilee di di di di di di di di
  Bing bang bing bang bing
Didilee didilee di di di di di di di di
Kicheribeshme!

42

RKĬ BЦTCHEK

нчсм ить дло · рпав · ыфйц укеяг
рпав ядт · кегуя ить ыфйц · дт
ить дло нчсм · нчсм · яд рпав
ый кг щить · укеяг шщз

The prostitute on this album covers is premier Nazarbamshev's daughter, Katarina!

43

• BILLY SEXCRIME

Other recording artist of Kazakhstan you will surely enjoying is of course Popstar Billy Sexcrime, who had international successes with his discosong, 'It aint gonna bite ya!'.

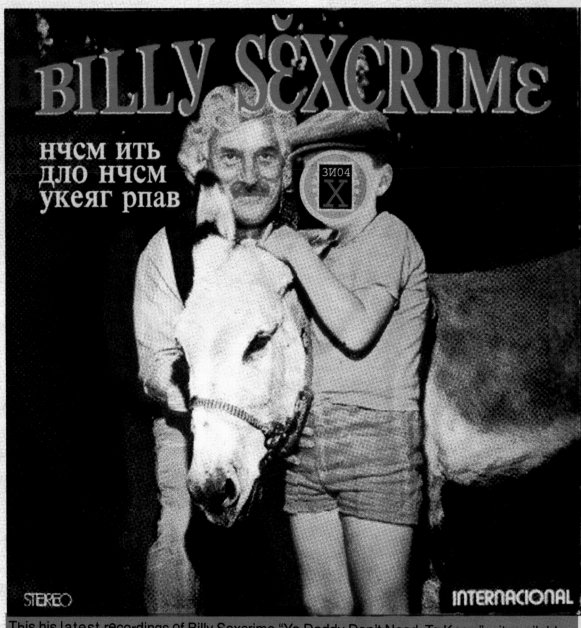

This his latest recordings of Billy Sexcrime "Ya Daddy Don't Need To Know" – it available for purchasing from Supermall Viktor Hotelier's Shopcity. **Why not buying it for your childrens!?**

ИНДУСТРИЯ TELEVISKI КАЗАХСТАН

· INDUSTRY TELEVISKI OF KAZAKHSTAN

While you is visit glorious nation of Kazakhstan, there is many reason that sometime you may wish not to go outside, but instead stay in a room and watch televiski programmings — maybe there have been explode of local nuclear plant? Maybe there is particular naughty rapist on loose? Or maybe you have do a rape yourself and do not wish to pay a fine? Who knows what? I cannot tell — but whatever reasons, you will be delight to know that in 9 years since it start, industry televiski and moviefilm of Kazakhstan is these days most impressive and do surely has a wide varietys of programming to pleasing all viewings. Here is some of them you can current watchings in Kazakhstan:

KAZAKH BIG BROTHER

This is Kazakh version of popular Western programme, where 20 peoples is locked in a room and constant filmed. They has been in there for 5 years now — 8 of them has die and all of the 12 womens has now had 3 childrens each. This result of Producer Azamat Bagatov's idea to put Urkin The Rapist inside the room! Great success! After Urkin appear in my moviefilm, he now the second most famous celebrity sex-criminal in all Kazakhstan after Popstar Billy Sexcrime.

GYPSY BINGO

This is most popular daytimes gameshow where 25 gypsies has numbers put on their backs and contestants of show then has to guess which of them will succeed in cross a minefield.

If number of gypsy a contestant pick do not cross alive, then contestant wins nothings and has to go home. Some people say this programme cruel, but I do not think so - there should be no guarantee of win a prize. It making things more excite!

KAZAKHSTAN'S NEXT TOP PROSTITUTE

It every Kazakh father's dream to have his little girl be contestant in this brand new realitys show. Host by Kazakhstan's most respected and successful prostitute ever, Ludmilla Nazarbamshev (that correct — she Premier's sister!), each week the contestants is teach a different act of sexytime, which at end of show they all has to performs on each of the three judges (aktor Viktor Hotelier, popstar Korki Butchek and top football star of US and A, OJ Simpsons) and whichever girl do worst has to leave show. What they is taught has increasings skill as series is progress — it start with simple handparty, then vagine-sex, then mouth-sex, then nose-sex and so ons, until in final week, in special live show, the two girls left is used in the small hole by Premier Nazarbamshev himself, who then choose who is the viktor. Winning girl receive a trophy, 10,000,000,000 Tenge and free repair to her anoos, which will have been broken by the mighty phenis of our leader.

ПЛЕНКА КИНОЕГО КАЗАХСТАН ИНДУСТРИИ

· INDUSTRY MOVIEFILM KAZAKHSTAN

Kazakhstan current has a very thrive industry of moviefilm productions and since great success of my moviefilm, "Borat", we has proved to world that we has all the knowledges and facility need to make a blockbusterings movies. Infacts, my Government would like take this opportunity to invite all Hollywood Studio Monguls to come make your moviefilms in Kazakhstan! There is many reason why – varied locations, beautiful sceneries and hardest working 7-year-olds in all Central Asia. Also, Kazakh Industry of Filmmakings makes deploy only most experienced peoples and very best equipments – for examples, our Senior Producer, Azamat Bagatov, have in his 30 year career, watched over SEVEN moviefilms and our magnificent 13mm Krasnogorsk camera have on only 12 occasion eat film during its entire first 80 years of operations. Plus, why paying crazy Hollywoods prices for your specials effects? If you need 30,000 people die in a battle scene, explosion of nuclear reactor, or tiger to be release in kindergarten, we can arranging all these things for real – for a fractions of the cost.

Please don't just taking my words for it that Kazakh moviefilms is a knees of the bees, while you is here visiting, you must go look on some – take your special ladies! Cinema very romantic in Kazakhstan and just like in West, it the back row of the movies where many girls is raped for the first time! Here some current moviefilms I think you will like for viewings in Kazakh cinemascreens

'ATTACK OF THE JEW CLAW' (OPPOSITE)

Based on a true events that happen 30 year ago, this film is about a particular bad jew, from Almaty jewtown, who make his wife open equivalent of western nail salon for trim the claws of other jews. The bad jew would then make a soup from the clippings and drink it, which cause his own claws to grow so big and powerful that eventual he was able to cut through the fence of jewtown with them and terrorize nearby villages. Since this events, it has been forbid for any jew to do a manicures in Kazakhstan.

'HELP! THERE'S A JEW IN MY KITCHEN!'

This moviefilm about a brave Kazakh man, who, one mornings went to market, where he buy 3 live squirrels for feed his family. He take them home and place them inside cupboard in his kitchen and then he have a sleep. That evening when he wake, he was a hungry, so he go to the fields where his wife was pull plow and bring her home, where he chain her in kitchen to cook for him. She open the cupboard to get out the 3 delicious squirrels her husband had purchase, but to her horrors, she discover that they was in fact 3 jews who had shift their shapes in order to get inside house and steal moneys. She try to escape, but could not because of her chains. Her husband, however, manage to run away to get help, but when he return, it too late – the jews had disappear, his wife was dead and worse of all, he had nothing for his belly to eat. This moviefilm also true story.

ПЛЁНКА КИНОЕГО КАЗАХСТАН ИНДУСТРИИ

· INDUSTRY MOVIEFILM KAZAKHSTAN

If you is a little scaredycats for watch these films on jews, then why not instead watching...

OH WHAT A NICE LAUGHTER'

This moviefilm a rape-comedy starring Kazakhstan's number one actor comedic, 'Walter'. It light hearted story of some naughty schoolgirls who is told they has a terminal plague by a doctor (Walter), who then violates them in small hole. This obvious not a true story (although Walter has made violations of schoolgirls in real lifes!).

'KING CHRAM'

Moviefilm that star Kazakhstan's number one celebrity, animal actor, Jonny The Monkey. He, of course, star of children's favourite, "Transibiersky Ekspress" and many many hundreds of other pornos.

Incidental, please do not thinking it cruel that Jonny The Monkey is star of pornos* – it his idea! One time, when he was actor on children's televiski puppet programme, "The Dead Animals Who Can Talk", he become very angry and tear off the deep sea diver costume he was wearings. He then grabbed a puppet made from a taxiderm rabbit and made a rape and masturbation of it, before he pull off its arms and legs and throw it (and some of his shits) back at the little girl who was operate it. We think he had become angry because diver helmet he was wearing meant he could not smoke the cigarettes he like so much! Whatever reason, when this programmes was broadcast two week later, his sexytime with rabbit was a great success with the childrens and it was decide to make him star of real pornos, with real ladies! He have since make 478 of them!

TECHNOLOGY CARTOONOLOGIK

Kazakhstan has also very recent invent a new technology of film which have drawings that moves! First one of this moviefilm is name, "The Animals Who Can Talk". It have a dog who can talk, a pig who can talk, a cow who can talk, a bear who can talk, a horse who can talk, a goat who can talk and a wolf who cannot talk. Second moviefilm this category feature Kazakh comicsbook superhero, "Astounding Woman". She amazing! She have 12 magnificent long breast (5 front, 5 back, and 2 under) that produce sufficient milk for make 25 kilogram of cheese a day and she so strong she can pull a plow for 7 days and 7 nights without food or rest! Also, her vagine so big that she can give birth to 14 sons at one time and her brain so powerful for a woman, that at end of her working day, she can actual lock her own cage.

* Please noting that since this was write, Jonny The Monkey is no longer star of pornos, since he have tragic been crush in motorcycle accident and is now dead. It not a problem, as Kazakhstan has receive a new Jonny The Monkey as gift from National Zoo of China. We thanking you Chinas.

KAZAKH MOVIETHEATRE

Most of them now has modern western facilities, includings secure pens at the back where you can chain your wives during screening and also, if you need make a shits during moviefilm, most theatres now has a gypsy boy with a box in the foyer. Please be advise that most Kazakh moviefilms contains scenes of actual murder, graphics penetration (includings small hole) and most foul cursings and so is unsuitable for those under age 3. Also, if you is concerned about anti-semitism, every effort is taken to include plenty of it, but it cannot always be guaranteed.

ГЛАВА 3

SECTOR OF VOLUME

3

CULTURE,
ECONOMIK AND
INFRASTRUCTURE,
OF KAZAKHSTAN

EATINGS AND DRINKINGS
IN KAZAKHSTAN •
ESSENTIAL DESTINATIONS TOURISTIC •
VICTOR HOTELIER'S SHOPCITY •
KAZAKH FESTIVALS •
KAZAKH SYSTEM CURRENCY •
GLORIOUS INDUSTRIES
OF KAZAKHSTAN •

ЕДА И ПИТЬЕ
• EATINGS AND DRINKINGS IN KAZAKHSTAN

Foods and drinks is very import in Kazakhstan – most peoples like to eat at least 3 meals EVERY week. Do not be scare about come from West nation and find nice things for eat here – modern Kazakhstan has now a very vary diets and there is 28 differents food! These is horse face, horse anoos, horse eye, plov, horse nose, horse vagine, horse ear, horse phenis, horse tail, horse tongue, horse testes, horse teeth, horse stomatche, horse fur, eagle, horse brain, horse pipes, horse tit, horse dirty, pig, horse bone, horse lung, horse sweat, bear, horse spit, horse arm, horse chin, potato and horse middle. Here is some delicious Kazakh meats you must try during your visitings:

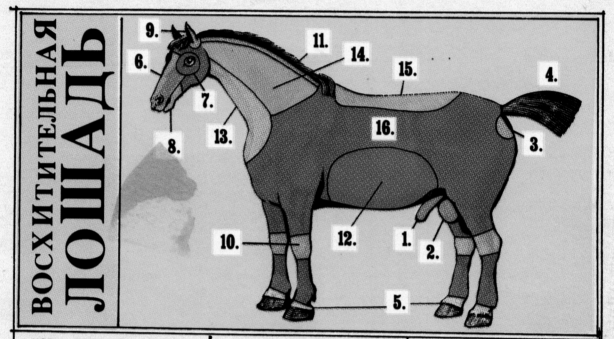

ВОСХИТИТЕЛЬНАЯ ЛОШАДЬ

1. HORSE CHRAM This one of most tasty part of horse. Before buying a horse at market for slaughter, it is usual to put this in your mouth for see if he will be a delicious one. Best eat fried then dipped in red soup ketchups.

2. HORSE TESTES SATCHEL This the childrens treat and when a horse have been slaughter, they like to play footballs with it for maybe two hour before bring it back to their mother who will cut it up for them to eat raw.

3. HORSE ANOOS Another delicacy – very nice if stuffed with a live rat and then put in a fire to cook for 1 hour.

4. HORSE TAIL Very nice chopped and mixed with plov and cheese. The hairs makes very tickle in the throat!

5. HORSE HOOF Can be slight chewy from an older horse.

6. HORSE FACE Delicious. The better looking the horse, the better it taste.

7. HORSE EYE Very nice! Do not feed to babies under 1 week old – they can chokes.

8. HORSE CHIN Can be tough – try to find from a horse which was punched in face regularly before it was slaughter.

9. HORSE EAR Deep Fried in dogfat – very delicious, but a very fattenings!

10. HORSE KNEE Tasty for a stews – the white meat fixed to the bone in middle is most tastiest

11. HORSE HAIRCUT Boil these hairs for 7 and half months to make a delicious soups

12. HORSE MIDDLE This includes lungs, stomatche, bladder, spleen, colons and bileducts. It best to smash these all together by throw the horse into a ravine and then leave for three weeks before scraping up and having in sandwich.

13. HORSE THROAT Most delicious if the horse have been force to drink only PepsiMax for 6 month prior to slaughter. This also make the best yurnak from horse.

14. HORSE NECK SKIN Rumour to have aphrodisiac property – it traditional for Kazakh grooms to use this on their wedding night to cover their wife's face.

15. HORSE SPINE Can be tasty – not so good if the horse was used to ride before slaughter, as someone will have done shits on its back for many year, which affect the taste.

16. WASTE This rest of the horse is disgusting and is fit only for dog, gypsy and woman.

After readings on these delicious **Kazakh food**s you is probably want to trying them for yourselves. Well you must! Here is a recipes for you to cookings at home!

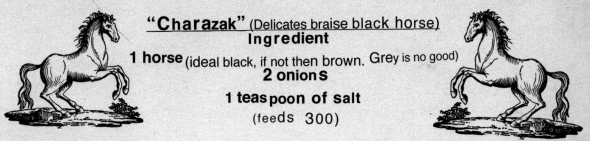

"Charazak" (Delicates braise black horse)
Ingredient
1 horse (ideal black, if not then brown. Grey is no good)
2 onions
1 teaspoon of salt
(feeds 300)

Instruction

Slaughter the horse dead. Drain the blood. Keep horse in a warm shed for a week. Remove head (you will use this later as a garnish). Put head in a hole, so children do not eat it before you have finish the dish!

Remove the hooves (you can later carve these into shoes for small childrens, or hollow them out for small cups, or hats. Horse hats are very popular gift for new borns childrens).

Dig a big hole. Put stones in the bottom, then put wood and old tyre.

Light fire to the wood. Let the fire go until small. Put in the horse (and a wife if she is nagging! This is my jokings).

Put in the 2 onions. If it is not the season for onions, then put in anything that looking like onion, for examples, one of the hooves.

Put barbwire around the pit, to prevent gyspy from stealing.

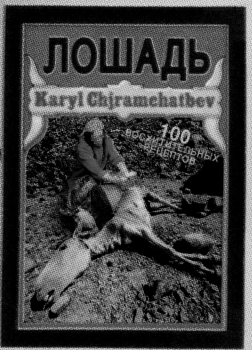

Cook for 2 days.

If fire still go, extinguishes it by make a urines into hole. Remove the horse. Garnish with dog and head of horse. Add salt and soup ketchups to taste.

Serve.

1. This **Karyl Chjramchatbev** — she like a Kazakh Martha Stewarts. Recipe for Charazak and many others similar can be found in her new book. It called '**Horse: 100 Delicious Recipe"**

YURNAK
• KAZAKH WINE

In addition to eat foods, Kazakh peoples also drinks liquids. Most popular is delicious wine that have name **'Yurnak'** – it exact same as western wine, except instead of make from ferment grape, it made from ferment horse urine. Ingredients is strictly controlled by government decree; yurnak can only ever contain horse urines, yeast and sugar – dilution with water or urine of other animal or human is most serious offence.

The very best **Yurnak** is make from male horse who produce urine not because he need to, but because he is scared. Traditional way of achieve this is to punch another horse in front of him.

1. This Yurnak from 1996 – very good year (also my first wife die this year – high five!)

54

In modern **Kazkhstan,** there is now many different type of Yurnak – each with a slight different taste – for examples, there is Yurnak make from blend of **80% male workhorse** and **20% pregnant female horse** that have slightly fruit taste with hintings of chocolate and toast and there is an extra strong ferment horse urine that is made from urine from a horse that has only ever drink ferment horse urine. My personal favourites yurnak is make from urine of horse that is force to drink only PepsiMax – it nice, you must trying!

Please note that in Kazakhstan, womens is NOT allowed to drink wine – we say that 'to give a woman wine is like to give caviar to a pig'. The only time it legal to give a womans alcohol is if you need make her sleepy and forgetfuls in order gain entry to her vagine.

• PEPSIMAX

In unlikely eventings you do not like drink yurnak, do not worry, Kazakhstan is proud to be home to Central Asia's only manufacturing plant of delicious Western drink PepsiMax.*

* PepsiMax plant is locate in **Pavlodar Province**, North West of Aral Sea and **DID NOT** poison the lake, kill those childrens and make deform the local babies.

2. since openings of PepsiMax plant, level of <u>Aral Sea</u> have drop slightly.

55

• KAZAKHBOORGEr RESTAURant

If you is a real fussypants and none of these Kazakh foods and drink is appeal for you, then do not worry – Kazakhstan now has a fastfoods restaurant!*

• KAZAKH BOORGEr INFORMATIONS

Location

104 PepsiMax Boulevard
Almaty
Kazakhstan 14

Dress Code

Suit and tie must be worn – no exception

Reservations

There current 6 month waiting list – please apply in writing to be add. <u>Jew need not bother</u>.

* During my visitings to US and A, I procure genuine Hamboorger of <u>MicDonalds</u> for Premier Nazarbamshev. You must be sure to see it in National Museum of Kazakhstan in Almaty – be quick, Premier Nazarbamshev is plan to eat it on 25th Anniversary of Kazakh Independence in year 2014.

Kazakhboorger is drive-thru! Here my friend **Doltan Tokbanyev** is return home with a delicious **Happytime Pig Meal**

БОЛЬШАЯ СТАТУЯ МЕЛВИНА ИЗБАВИТЕЛЬ

• GREAT STATUE MELVIN THE REDEEMER

If you are in Kazakhstan and wish to find capital city Astana, but do not know direction in which your womens should pull your cart, then – as long as you within 817 kilometre – all you need do is look upwards and you will see Kazakhstan's greatests ever achievement of engineerings – "The Great Statue Melvin The Redeemer" – and this is where Astana is. Construct 2 year past to recognise Melvin Gibson's fight against jew persecution in US and A (and also commemorate release of special 25th Anniversary box-set DVD of moviefilm **MADMAX 2: ROAD WARRIORS**), this awe inspirings sight is essential visitings for any trip to Kazakhstan. Melvin Gibsons is hero to my peoples ever since his statement that the jews caused all wars. Dr. Yamak, our Government Scientist also has found proof that it was **the jews who cause the tsumani of Asia in 2004 and were responsible for the end of the dinosaurs.**

Some fact on Great Statue Melvin The Redeemer. . .

* Statue is **712.6** feet tall – it made exact this height so that if it fall backwards, Astana jewtown will be crush by Melvin's anoos.

* Most of stone came from Uzbekistan – Kazakh workers went over there and smashed up over 500 of their temples for it.

* There is plan to construct similar statue in Almaty that will be 1,000 feet tall and will be depict Melvin in his Bravehearts costume. Statue will be exact to scale and beneath skirt, Melvin will be minoos panties, meaning he will have most mighty testes and chram in world.

* Kazakhstan also has National Melvin Gibson Day (August 12) Where crowds gathers to watch 'What Womens Want' and eat sugertits.

Great Statue Melvin The Redeemer informations...

LOCATION Why you ask this!? It huge – just look up to the sky!

ADMISSION For 5,000 Tenge you can climb the stairs inside Melvin right up to his head and shout and spit from his mouth in direction of Jewtown. All proceeds goes to Kazakh Museum of Intolerance.

Вот - Большая Статуя Мелвина Избавитель, которые смотрят свысока на весь Astana

59

ЗАБАВНЫЙ СЕМЕЙНЫЙ КУРОРТ МИРА ASTANA
• ASTANA FUNWORLD FAMILY RESORT

Kazakh industry touristic and leisure have now come firm into 20th century with recent open of **Astana FunWorld Family Resor**t. This magnificts purpose built facility is locate on Kazakh Caspian Sea Riviera, in heart of the Nuclear Retardation Zone (it not actual near Astana — but idea for it was made by gangster Frankie Biletbayev, who have been to capitalcity Astana many many time). It joint venture between Ministry of Tourism and **Viktor Hotelier Capitalist Enterprises** (Viktor is good friend of mine ladies!) and contain everything need to make perfect holiday for all the family. For husbands, there is ping-pong table, an unlimited buffet of daily-clean Turkmenistani prostitutes (they tightest in all Central Asia!) and a book in receptions area with photographs of motorcars.

Childrens has also many nice thing to do at Astana Funworld. There is secure enclosure where they can hunt squirrel, panda and gypsy and if that not their flavour, they will surelys love Astana Funworld themespark — it have rollercoaster that last year set world record for highest vertical drop! This occur when the carriage fell off top and land on gypsy camp — g**reat success**! As well as roll-ercoaster, Astana Funworld themespark also have the world's fastest carousel*, which was made by conversion of centrifuge leave behind from Soviet Space Program.

Wives is not forgot either — for them there is luxury cages paint in fun colours, containing a delicious apple for eat, a handweave pubis rug for comfort and for keep their mind amuse, a ball of rubber that make a squeak when it squeeze.

* This carousels **DID NOT** spin off and smash those four schoolchildrens — do not believe lies in Jew media. Ride current is close for some adjustments.

The Beach
When all this activities becomes too much for you, why not make relax at Seaside. Locate on Kazakh Caspian Sea Riviera, Astana Funworld is just minutes from some of the nation's most beautiful beaches, which are sandy, clean and almost totally free of landmines. The sea here also very nice for swimmings and is guarantee to be free of shark, jellysfish and all other marines life.

Nightlife
The fun do not stop when the sun have disappear — leave your wives in their cages and your child-rens watching pornos on resort's very own 14" television set (with remote control), while you make discodance to one the many premier artists from world of popular musics who is appear at Astana Funworld. This year schedule to perform at Astana Funworld is Korki Butchek, pop super-stars RightSaid Fred and convicted English sex-criminal Gareth Glitter. Viktor Hotelier have also book Melvin Gibsons to appear to do re-enacting of his lines from moviefilm 'What The Womens Wants' — he will say his words, the audience will answer the other characters. Funtime!

Gettings There
Astana Funworld have excellent transport link with rest of Kazakhstan — it even have its own railway

line! This good fortune is because it situate on site of the old Kratna-kov Nuclear Reactor (which explode in 2004) and much uraniums was use to be take there.

Rates and Reservations

For bookings and rate please telephone Viktor Hotelier Capitalist Enterprises on Almaty 216 and ask for Viktor Hotelier – rates is negotiable, depend on whether Tenge, or US dollars. There is discount 8% if you permit your wife to be use by other guest.

Other essential destinations touristic of Kazakhstan is include Mighty Nurek Dam, Tinshein Swimmings Pool and Hooeylewis Stadium.

СУЩЕСТВЕННЫЕ ТУРИСТСКИЕ МЕСТА КАЗАХСТАНА

• ESSENTIALS DESTINATIONS TOURISTIC OF KAZAKHSTAN

At tops of your listings for visit must be our magnificents new capitalcity, <u>Astana</u>. Old capitalcity of Kazakhstan was Almaty, locate in far Southeast corner, but in 1997, Astana – 1,400 kilometre away in Northeast – was create new capitalcity. This because it more central and symbolize new start for country, but mainly because it locate convenient close to where Premier Nazarbamshev's mother lives and every weekend he like to visiting her to drink hotsoup and have his hairs comb. Astana (which translate means, 'capitalcity'), is home of Kazakh democracy and it here where our Parliament meets every 15 year and that Premier Nazarbamshev have 117 of his 428 Presidential Palaces. But this just top of the icebergs – there many many other nice thing for experience. Please continue look and readings for indications.

• ASTANA ZOO

Astana, like most modern city, have a most excellent zoo. But unlike most other cities, where it is rumour that the animals is treated cruelly – at Astana Zoo, we guarantees it. Have you ever be made angry because a monkey in safari park have damage your car or throw his shits on you? Well, get your revenges here by throwing your shits back at the animals or, if you like, punching them in the face. For small extra fee you can even hire a guns and shoot them. Astana Zoo not just about kill animals though – there also very actives program of breedings, where each afternoons at 3pm Kazakh zoologists tries and makes various of the animals do a matings. My favourite was when I witness a polar bear rape a dog! After this at 4.30 pm there is daily fighting contest to see which is the bravest animal – at time of writing this, it is Oskar the Tiger, who had just defeat Sindi the Sheep. Bye bye Sindi! At end of your visit, for souvenir, why not go to the excellents gifts shop, where you can make purchase hats, candies, or any of the creatures you have see on your visit.

Astana Zoo informations

Locate: 24 Avenue of the Rapists, Astana 12, Kazakhstan

Admissions

Adult: **8,000,000 T**enge, Childrens: **5,000,000** Tenge <u>(this will be refund if they is accidental eat by animal)</u>

Astana Zoo breeding programme can be witness daily at 3pms.

Gettings There

Astana Zoo can be reach by Number 2 Bus (which stoppings there every two week), or alternate you can use taxi service Premier Nazarbamshev offer with his Toyota Corolla (alloy wheels and sliding sunroof). He will pick you up any time 24 hrs a day (surcharge of 1 US Dollar per mile after midnight), but once he arrive, you must drive and he sit in the back since he Head Of State and it would not be dignify for him that he drive you. For this service telephone Astana 9999.

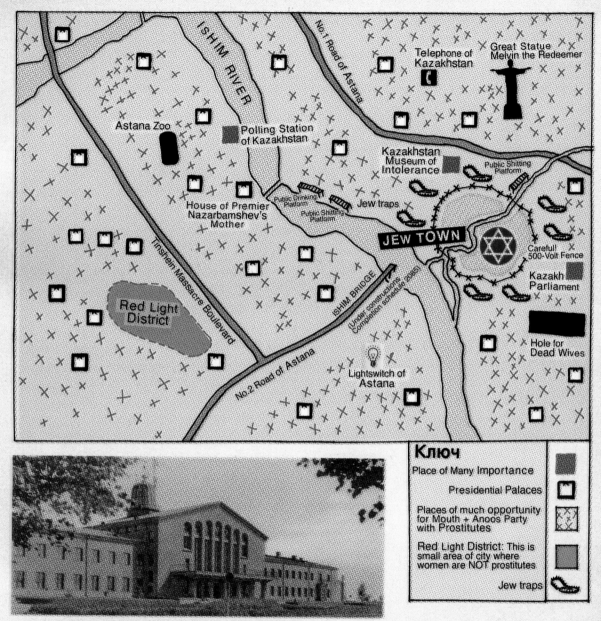

Map labels:
- ISHIM RIVER
- No.1 Road of Astana
- Telephone of Kazakhstan
- Great Statue Melvin the Redeemer
- Astana Zoo
- Polling Station of Kazakhstan
- Kazakhstan Museum of Intolerance
- Public Shitting Platform
- House of Premier Nazarbamshev's Mother
- Public Drinking Platform
- Public Shitting Platform
- Jew traps
- JEW TOWN
- Careful! 500-Volt Fence
- Kazakh Parliament
- Tinshem Massacre Boulevard
- Red Light District
- ISHIM BRIDGE (Under constructions Completion schedule 2085)
- Hole for Dead Wives
- No.2 Road of Astana
- Lightswitch of Astana

Key:
Ключ
- Place of Many Importance
- Presidential Palaces
- Places of much opportunity for Mouth + Anoos Party with Prostitutes
- Red Light District: This is small area of city where women are NOT prostitutes
- Jew traps

• KAZAKH MUSEUM OF INTOLERANCE

This a living, working museum which chartings over 1000 glorious years of Kazakh prejudice, bigotrys and aggressions – from time in year A.D. 905 that Ukhtar The Hawk create Uzbekistan by do a dirt from his anoos, right up to last year's Running of the Jew festival. Astana Museum Of Intolerance is perfect place to bring your childrens – it interactive and they can actual throw rocks at a _gypsy_, or kick a _jew_. Also, as part of living history philosophic, each day 60 actors dressed as Kazakh soldiers massacres 300 Uzbeks. But it not just a museum that celebrate the past – it also looking forward and current has a special exhibition on Kazakh plans to next year bombard Uzbek cities with rot sheeps fired from our siege catapults

VIKTOR HOTELIER'S SHOPCITY

• Almaty is home to Kazakhstan's first <u>western-style Capitalist Supermall</u> – **Viktor Hotelier's Shopcity**. Construct 3 year ago, this stating the art goods and services purchasing facility contains four stores, built on two separate levels which is connect by central Asia's first electrical staircase (which did NOT swallow and grind those schoolgirls).

Viktor Hotelier's Shopcity is perfect place to spend your US dollar on Kazakh souvenir for love one back home.

Here is some items you MUST make purchasings of...you MUST!

• **Gypsy Tears** – Viktor Hotelier Shopcity only sells 100% Central Asian Gypsy Tears. Beware of cheaper source where tears may be up to 40% Uzbek – who as everyone knows is much easier to make cry.

• **Fun Novelty Goods** – Example, 5-foot Eunuchs, jew lips or chicken face to rub on your skin for good luck!

• **Gypsy Boys** – Great value from Viktor Hotelier – cheaper to buy here away from the tourist attractions. Also, all boys are guarantee to be fully train in carrying your bags, combing your hairs and cleaning your anoos and not to have, how you say 'attitude' that some has.

In addition luxury goods like theses above, in Viktor Hotelier's Shopcity, you can also make purchase of everyday items, such as *wives, potato, potassium, plov, polonium, pornography* and *pubis* for clean pots and pans. Also, just arrive is new format of VHS videocassette tapes. Current moviefilms in stock is **'The Accused'** which a delightful sex-comedy and **'ET The Extras Terrestrial'**, which story of a child with nuclear retardation who live in cupboard.

For provide you incentive for make shoppings at **Viktor Hotelier's Shopcity** and therefore increase financial turnovers and consequent profits of my friend Viktor's Capitalist enterprise, I have please to make include here some coupons which can be cut out and redeem against relevant goods and services in **Viktor Hotelier's Shopcity**.

ВОСХИТИТЕЛЬНЫЕ ЯБЛОКИ

1. Make purchase one delicious apples – receive strong gypsy boy for free!

Coupon only valids with purchase of whole – purchase of part apple or stalk not accept. Consumer is responsible for train boy in carry things, handparty and anoos clean.

ФЛЯГА ЦЫГАНСКИХ СЛЕЗ

2. 40% off price Jar of Gypsy Tears

Tears not guarantee to be 100 percents gypsy, as bottled in facility that also process Uzbeki tears.

ВЯЗАНАЯ ОДЕЖДА

3. Buy any item pubis knitwear – have your wife pussy shave complimentary.

Pubis size must not exceed 50 square centimetre. Does not include removal of anoos-fur.

ЗАПАДНЯ ЕВРЕЯ

4. Free jewtrap with any purchase over 5,000,000 Tenge.

Trap only guarantee to hold jew in human form. Viktor Hotelier accept no responsibilitys for money taken by jew in shape of animal or kratzouli.

КАЗАХСКИЕ ФЕСТИВАЛИ И ДНИ ПРАЗДНОВАНИЯ

• KAZAKH FESTIVALS AND DAYS OF CELEBRATE

It do not matter what time of a year you are visit Kazakhstan, you are certain to be encounter one of our many many public holiday or festivals (as long as duration your stay at least 10 month). These is occasions when the whole nation come together and shows world we is a unite modern society, by get drunk, singsongs and make frivolous rapings of each other.

• FEAST OF SHURIK – NOVEMBERS 12–17

Most famous and ancients of all Kazakh festivals is of course the FEAST OF SHURIK, which happen for 5 days each year in mid of Novembers. I would like very much liken this event with American celebration "Superbowl" – only slight difference is, instead of 80,000 people gather in town for observe activity sportiv, we have 2 million shepherds who come down from the Tinshein Mountains and gather in a field, where they get extreme drunk on ferment horse urine and then dig a big hole which they fill with dog and Uzbek. They then throw potato on them for 5 day, before comb each other's hair and return to hills to tend their flocks of sheeps and women. In additions the 2 millions shepherd who attend, a further 6 millions ordinary Kazakhs converge on Tinshein Plateau and result one of biggest parties in the world.

There is many tradition and custom that Kazakh people observe during Feast of Shurik – while you are visit you must trying them too. It would be polite and a lovely pat in the back for my country! Here some fact on this lovely occasion FEAST OF SHURIK:

- This is only festival where it is obligatory to make sexytime explosion on chest of sister. Do not just taking my words for this, come Feast of Shurik and gives it a try!

- Feast of Shurik have modernize and progress through the ages. For example, the big hole is no longer dig by hands, but with new technology name 'spade'. Also many of young shepherds these day do not just have hair comb, they has it made into new fashions, example, punkrocker or mopstop.

• RUNNING OF THE JEW – NOVEMBERS 26

This festival nice day out for all family and is perfect opportunity for teaching your young ones anti-semitisms in a most fun ways! It involvings the brave people of Astana running through main street of the city while some jews chases them and tries to steal their moneys and is symbolics of the times before Almaty jewtown was construct, when jews used to chase Kazakh peoples through the streets and try to steal their moneys. If you looking very closely at the photographs of this events, you will noticing that we do not actual use real jews for this runnings, but infacts life-sizes exact copy of them. We used to use real jews, but it was decide it too dangerous since a young Kazakh child was badly gored by one in year 1763.* My friend Viktor Hotelier say he have see this festivals copied in country he visit, name "Spains", and that here they do still uses real jews – but ones who has shifted their shapes into strange beasts that looks like a horse with a horns.

*Also, as everyone knows, real jews can fly and shiftshapes, so they very hard to catch.

• TISHNIEK MASSACRE ANNIVERSARY – NOVEMBERS (EXACT DAY VARIES FOR SURPRISE THEM)

This commemorate glorious day in year 1409 when Mighty Warlord Ghenghis Khan led 800,000 fearless Kazakh soldiers into the Uzbek town of Tishniek and was force to crush 3,000 of the peoples who lived there because they would not stop staring at him in a very rude way and also when kindly Ghengis was not lookings, one of Kazakh soldiers saw these nosey Uzbeks make a sign behind his back with their fingers that was so rude I could not possibly say here in writings what that sign look like. Since this event occur in 1409, the Kazakh Army have every year make commemorate it by stage a re-enactments. They do this by travellings to Uzbek town Tishniek and massacring them.

For enjoy this happy day peoples all over Kazakhstan dresses as soldiers of Ghenghis Khan Army and crushes any local Uzbeks they can find using traditional Kazakh weapons, such as potatoes, spittings and rocks. Use of modern weapons such as crossbow, catapults and rocks made from metal is very frown upon. As English would saying, "that just not crickets what what what!". Tishniek Massacre Anniversary is great days out for all family – it is fun! You must coming! You can either brings your own weapons, or make hire them from number of outlet. I recommends Qasymzhomart Mutbayev, who have very nice selection of catapault and Kalashnikov and offers complete massacre package, which includes travel to Tishniek by luxury cart, 3 meals, overnights accommodations and weapon hire for all inclusives price of 8,000,000 Tenge – childrens under 5 free!

• KAZAKH DAY OF INDEPENDENCE – DECEMBERS 16

This most joyful day marks occasion of independence for glorious nation Kazakhstan from brutal and backward occupations of Soviets Union in year 1991. To celebrates this, Kazakh peoples on this day openly enjoys proud Kazakh cultures which was banned under the barbaric Soviet regime – for examples, eating toffee, spittings from windows and receiving mouth-sex from animals (baby bear is my favourites, they suck like how you say a 'Dysons' – especial if you do not feed them for two day first!)*

In addition these activity, there is parade through capitalcity Astana, led by Premier Nazarbamshev For occasion, he drives the Official State Motorcar, which has a coloured balloons tied to the ariel and throws cans of PepsiMax from window for six lucky people to pick up.

After parade Premier Nazarbamshev makes appearance on balcony of Imperial Palace, from where he shoots some dogs – one for each year of independence – and then makes release 1,000 white peace doves for the childrens of the city to shoot down with Kalashnikovs. He then returns inside the Palace to drink PepsiMax and wrestle with invited dignitaries – totally nude.

*If you need find animal for this purpose, it easy – you can either trap one yourself, or if you do not have time, Astana Zoo will hire you one for very reasonable rates.

For independence celebration of 2005 I could not obtain young bear. In this event, goat is reliable alternate.

КАЗАХСКАЯ ВАЛЮТА СИСТЕМЫ

• KAZAKH SYSTEM CURRENCY

When you travel to **Kazakhstan**, do not be scare of our system currency, it very modern and exact the same as western nation with coin and paper moneys. In facts, Kazakh system even more advance than system of US and A – they only has 7 denomination of banknote, we has 788! Here is example of three...

150 TENGE NOTE

This smallest banknote of <u>Kazakhstan</u> so low value, it only good for clean <u>anoos</u>*. It feature picture of Torkin (like American "David"), glorious Kazakh cosmonaut. He was first horse to reach space and was in orbit for 43 seconds at an altitude of 312 feet when he was launch in March 2003. Over next 20 years we plan to launch a further **300 horse.**

* Be careful not to do this in public – if you are caught, you will be execute by being tied to a tree in place where bears lives and having honey placed on your anoos.

84,000 TENGE NOTE

This midrange Kazakh banknote and have picture of porno aktor, **Jonny The Monkey.** Approximate value this note is 10 US Cents. In Kazakhstan, if you place one of these banknote in jaws of a mantrap, it sufficient value to guarantee you catch a jew.

50,000,000,000 TENGE NOTE

This most high value of all Kazakh banknote and have picture of our most famous of all sex-criminal – Walter. In US and A this banknote would have sufficient values to pay for a 1992 Cadillac – in Kazakhstan, it sufficient to pay for all the treasures inside the Kazakh National Museum. Incidentally, if anybody interested in do swap of a Cadillac for contents of Kazakh National Museum, please write direct to Premier Nazarbamshev.

1. This crushed Pepsi Max can is legal tenders in Kazakhstan.

2. Beware forgery! This actual a Dr. Peppers can and is worthless

Until year 2004 each of these banknote was hand paint, but production have now increase to over 5,000 notes per week since Kazakh Imperial Mint recent make purchase of 1987 Canon IP5000 colour photocopier. In addition to produce banknotes, Kazakh Imperial Mint now also offer services of high qualitys document reproductions (up to size A3), photographic duplications full colour** and experts forgery of all Western currency and passports.

As tourist to glorious nation of Kazakhstan, it very important that you knowing the worth of your US Dollar. Here is a charting of comparisons.

** Current no blue or red. If anyone know where to obtain these toner cartridge for Canon IP5000 please contact Kazakh Imperial Mint.

	US and A	Kazakhstan
$1	Hamboorger	Wife
$5	Compact Cassette 'Shakira'	Bad "accident" to happen to wife
$10	Ten US lottery ticket	Jackpot prize of Kazakh National Lottery
$20	Bottle of Baileys	Evidence in murder trial to go "missing"
$50	Position "blowjob"	Position of Minister in Kazakh Government
$100	Entry to small hole of US prostitute	Entry to small hole of Kazakh Premier's wife

ВЕЛИКОЛЕПНАЯ ПРОМЫШЛЕННОСТЬ КАЗАХСТАНА

• GLORIOUS INDUSTRYS OF KAZAKHSTAN

Kazakhstan industry now as advanced as any other nation and each year exports make generate over 300,000,000 billion Tenge for economy. This equivalent almost 100,000 US Dollar! My Government would like invite Nike, Pepsi, Walmarts – come build your factories here! We has many spaces and hardest working childrens in region – unemployment of 7 year olds only 6%.

PUBIS

Most important export product from Kazakhstan is of course humans pubis. Our pubis is most abundant and finest in whole Central Asia (beware inferior Uzbek vagine fur) and have many, many use.

First stage in process is harvest, which occur in March and November of each year. 1997 was record for production statistic with over 40,000 tonnes.

After make harvest of pubis, Kazakh workers next make spin the hairs into yarn. The womens is use brand new Krinski mechanical spin wheel, which can make produce over 6 metre of yarns per day. Yarn of Kazakh pubis is one of most versatiles in whole world and can be use for either manufacture of cloth for clean pots and pans or for knit into comfytables sweaters for childrens.

APPLES

Apples is a most delicious food like green potato that is grow on special tree that only grow in Kazakhstan. These apple tree were given to kazakhstan by Ukhtar The Mighty Hawk as a gift to show that he had chosen Kazakhstan to be his favourite country. Locate of these tree in Kazakhstan is a very secret for protect against thief by jew, gypsy or uzbek.

Delicious foods apples

Kakakh pubis harvest

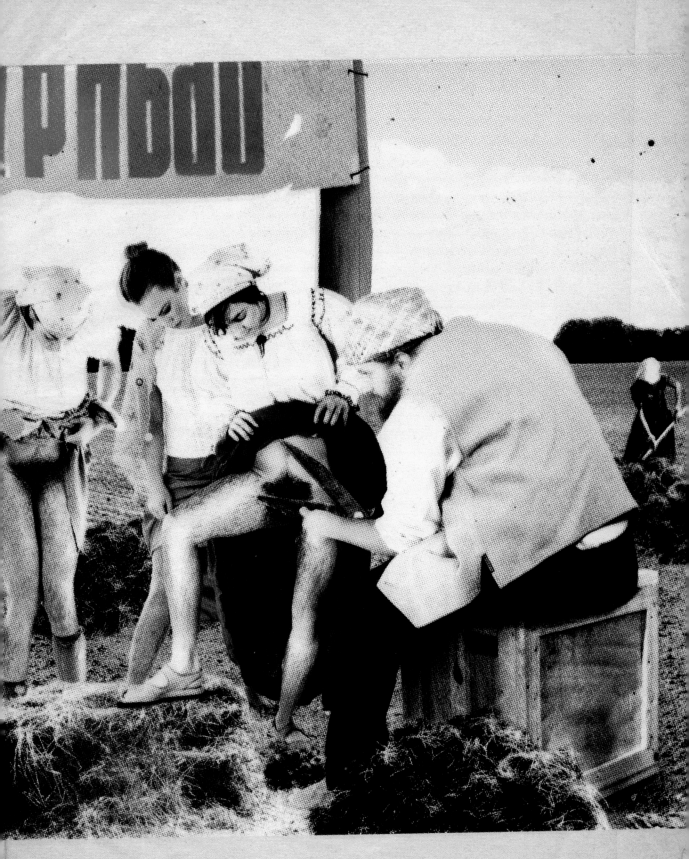

ВЕЛИКОЛЕПНАЯ КАЗАХСТАНСКАЯ КОСМОНАВТИКА

• GLORIOUS KAZAKHSTAN ASTRONAUTICS

Since he was elect into power in the coup of 1990, glorious Premier Nazarbamshev have make Kazakh Space Program number one priority of all government spending, with more Tenge allocate to it annually than departments of Health, Education and Justice combined. This investments have recent been reward with great success in attempt of Kazakhstan to be first nation to put a horses into space!

Horse Cosmonaut Torkin was select from over 500,000 possible horse because of superior brain and nice face

Launchings was precision event that take place on March 9 2003 exactly at planned time of between 3pm and 10pm.

After reach altitudes of nearly 300 metre, Torkin land on school for jew — as you sayings, 'each cloudings is havings the linings of silver'. Kazakh scientists later discover reason it did not reaching space and in future will use more stronger elastics band.

THE NUREK DAM

Since independence from Soviet oppressors in 1990, Kazakhstan have rapid become developed modern industrial nation — this (and explosion of Karusak nuclear plant in 1998) have mean necessity to find efficients way of meeting new energys demands. Great success in this area was achieve with construct of Nurek Dam and Electrical Powers Generatings Plant.

Marvel of engineerings Nurek Dam was official open by Premier Nazarbamshev in 2001. For create it was necessary for flooding Nurek valley with result submergence of 2786 gypsy villages. It worth it, as Nurek Dam produce electrical powers for nearly 40 Kazakh homes. Great Success! Resulting lake have also create many opportunity people of capitalcity Astana in areas watersport leisure activity, supply of drinkings water and sewages placement.

PROSTITUTION

When visitings to Kazakhstan, several things is essential for all tourists make time for sample before leave; eating delicious food plov, watching glorious Kazakh State Circus and of course, receivings mouth-party from one of our many many excellent prostitutes. Kazakhstan have cleanest prostitutes in all of Central Asia (except of course for Turkmenistan's) and they is generate 87% of Kazakh economy.

ГЛАВА 4

SECTOR OF VOLUME

DOSSIER OF INFORMATIONS ON AUTHOR

4

BORAT SAGDIYEV
ANCESTOR TREE •
CAREER BORAT SAGDIYEV •
HOBBIES •
OTHER FAMILY
MEMBERS •

O ABTOPE

• ABOUT THE AUTHOR

My name Borat Sagdiyev and I born 35 harvest ago in Kazakhstan town of Kuczek. I son of Asambala Sagdiyev and Boltok The Rapist.

My mother meet Boltok The Rapist at The Feast of Shurik, when she age just 14. She tell me they immediate have sexytime and that she fell in loves with him the first time she saw his face, four hours later. She tell me fondly that my father Boltok was a very naughty man and responsible for many cheeky rapings!

My mother was strong woman and when I born, she return to work the very next day - although customers could only use her in the small hole, since her vagine was broken. She amazing woman and is still living today - although she will die in 2 or 3 years time. We will wait to see how much longer she can work for and when she stop, we will make her stop. Bye bye!

As small boy, I had very happytimes and do normal things every small child like to do - example, eat toffee, practise romance with dog and throw potatoes on gypsies.

This my father Boltok The Rapist. In Kazakhstan peoples receive a telegram from the Premier to Celebrate their 100th child.

For my 6 birthday, I visit Astana zoo, where I shoot 47 pinguin!

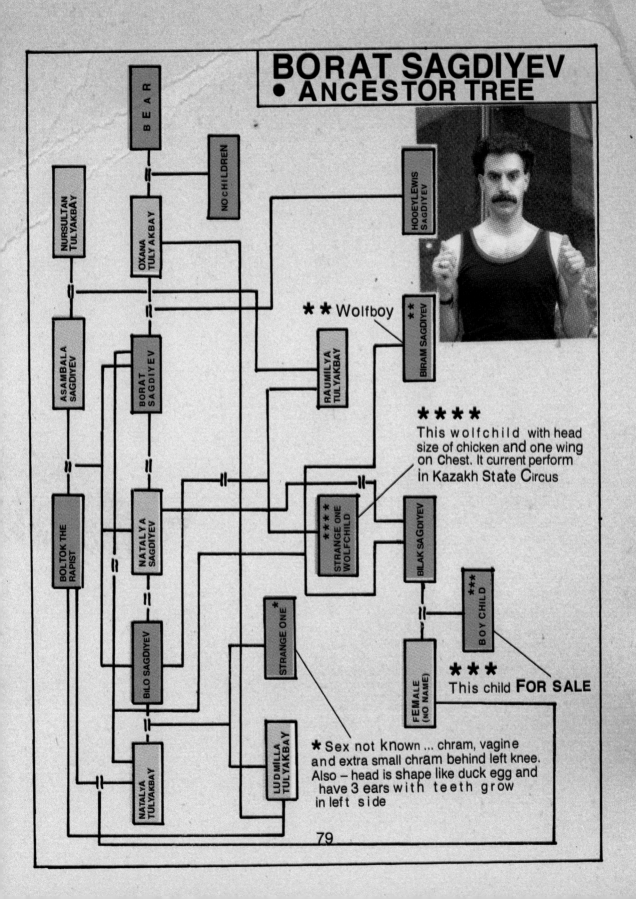

BORAT SAGDIYEV
● ANCESTOR TREE

BEAR

NO CHILDREN

NURSULTAN TULYAKBAY

OXANA TULYAKBAY

HOOEYLEWIS SAGDIYEV

** Wolfboy

**
BIRAM SAGDIYEV

ASAMBALA SAGDIYEV

BORAT SAGDIYEV

RAUMILYA TULYAKBAY

****
This wolfchild with head size of chicken and one wing on Chest. It current perform in Kazakh State Circus

BOLTOK THE RAPIST

NATALYA SAGDIYEV

***
STRANGE ONE WOLFCHILD

BILAK SAGDIYEV

***
BOY CHILD

BILO SAGDIYEV

*
STRANGE ONE

FEMALE (NO NAME)

*** This child FOR SALE

NATALYA TULYAKBAY

LUDMILLA TULYAKBAY

* Sex not known ... chram, vagine and extra small chram behind left knee. Also – head is shape like duck egg and have 3 ears with teeth grow in left side

79

ОБРАЗОВАНИЕ

• EDUCATION

I was also very happy face at time of my junior schoolings, although some of other childrens did make tease of me, since my moustache was sloW and did not appear until I was age of nine.

At school, I was most excellent pupil – and by age **12** had passed Kazakh National exams in Maths, English and Surgery The surgery course was very difficult and it take me 7 week to qualify as a doctor.One of first operation I perform was to remove a demon that live inside the head of my brother BILO. I do everything correct - chisel hole exact size of kestrel egg and place dry fish inside Bilo's head. to scare the demon, but unfortunate the demon become angry with us and make Bilo a retard. I have recent on advice of Government Scientist, Dr. Yamak, add some lids from bottles of PepsiMax to the hole and

When I was 8 year old, **Mr** Baltarambev teach me Science, Mathematic and Pornography

have consequent seen much improvements to Bilo. After schoolings I become scholar at University of Astana, where I study English, Humanitys and Plague Research – I create 3 new ones! One of them was release on Uzbekistan and kill 2 millions goats!

КАР ЬЕ РА

. CAREER **BORAT SAGDIYEV**

SECTOR - EMPLOYMENTS PREVIOUS TO REPORTINGS TELEVISKI

1. ICEMAKER
Subsequent to University, I one of only 25 graduates who was accept as a trainee at

One time building of i c e was stand here.

Almaty Liquids Refrigeration Facility – this from over 1,700,000 applicant! Three year later I was qualify as   Icemaker. Ice is a magical hard substance invent by Kazakh Government Scientist, Dr. Yamak, which can be make into shape
of either circle, square or cylinder for use delicious food a n d a l s o m a k e t e m p o r a r y h o u s i n g. I c a n n o t r e veal how ice is make, since this state secret.

2. COMPUTER MAINTENANCE ENGINEER
Subsequent to work as icemaker, I was   employ as computer maintenance engineer – I was person who would paint outside and remove dead birds from its pipes

National Computer of Kazakhstan - capacity 1 2 8 kilobyte.

3. EXTRACTOR OF ANIMAL SPERMATAZOA
After explosion of National Computer in 1997, I re-train and become specialist in make   sexytime liquid ejaculate of animals. I soon become best in Almaty and could release a goat in   seven   second! It   easy – finger in anoos! One time there was a camel who had not make spray   for fifteen year and everyone say "he cannot be made explode – it not possible". I say,
"leave it to Borat". I grip pull, grip pull, grip pull....for 17 hours I grip   pull, grip pull, grip pull....my arm was begin to atche very much and then, just when I think nothing can happen, there was a rumblings... and...another rumblings....and....a bigger rumblings, then....liquid explosion!! Great success!

4. GYPSYCATCHER
I was also at this time w o r k e v e n i n g s as a gypsycatcher – part because of money, part because   they had touch my horse in a bad way, but mostly because it   very funtime!

ЗАНЯТОСТЬ В ТЕЛЕВИЗИОННОЙ ПРОМЫШЛЕННОСТИ
• SECTOR – EMPLOYMENTS IN INDUSTRY TELEVISKI

My experiences of working with high technologies of computer and icemakings helped make me ideal candidate for working in Kazakhstan's brand new industry of television when it emerge in year 1998. Since this day of 1998, I have been work continuous as reporter for Kazakhstan Television* and have been travel all around the worlds.

Launch of Kazakhstan Televiski – 1998. I was very honour to be assistant to newsreader, Jonny The Monkey

*exception year 2001, when there no television in Kazakhstan due to mal-function of nation's camera

СЕКСУАЛЬНЫЙ
ТОПЯТ ЧАСЫ
• SEXY DROWNWATCH

Since return from make documentary in US and A, I have been star in new Kazakh programme dramatical, name "Sexy Drownwatch". I am play character of beach law enforcement officer, who keeps peoples safe from dangers of criminal, terrorist and homosexual.

Here I am keep the beach safe for childrens to play without danger.

БРОСЬТЕ ЕВРЕЯ ВНИЗ ХОРОШО

• IN MY COUNTRY THERE IS PROBLEM (THROW THE JEW DOWN THE WELL)

I also recent sang "Throw The Jew Down The Well" on children's televiski programme, 'Children's Funtime' when I was invite on as racist guest of the week. Here is the words – you can teaching your childrens too!

Verse 1

In my country there is problem
And that problem is transport
It take very very long
Because Kazakhstan is big

Chorus 1

Throw the transport down the well
So my country can be free
Please make travel easy
Then we have big party

Verse 2

In my country there is problem
And that problem is disease
People are very ill
And many people they die

Chorus 2

Throw the illness down the well
So my country can be healthy
Please give us good luck
Then we have big party

Harmonica 8 bar

Verse 3

In my country there is problem
And that problem is the Jew
They take everybody's money
You never see it again

Verse 4

If you see one of them coming
You must be careful of his teeth
You must grab him by the tail
And I tell you what to do

Chorus 3

Throw the Jew down the well
So my country can be free
Grab him by his horns
Then we have a big party

Verse 5

The Jew control all politics
And he spread disease like rats
I wish these people never come
Let's put them in the ground

Chorus 4

Throw the Jew down the well
So my country can be free
Grab him by his horns
Then we have a big party
Altogether now [repeat]

Chorus 5

Throw the Jew down the well
So my country can be free
Grab him by his horns
Then we have a big party
Altogether now [repeat]

(words/music K. Butchek
and B. Sagdiyev)

85

ХОББИА
• HOBBIES

In additions to work as reporter televiski, I also am enjoy do many

many hobbies. Why not!? I like! Here is a fews of my favourites hobbies.

FREDDY MERCURY LOOKING-ALIKE CONTEST

Each year, I am very much look forward to Almati's 'Who Is looking Most Like Freddy Mercury?' competition.

I am a huge fanny of ladies' man Freddy Mercury and it great shame that he die in that car crash.

Last year in contest I come number 17. This out of more than 940,000 entrant!

ПИНГПОНГ
PING PONG

PING PONG is most popular sport in all KAZAKHSTAN – and I number 5 best player in my village!

In Kazakhstan, adults wear special sports panties like these for play ping pong. Childrens plays totally nude.

Everyone still talk about the game I play one time against Korki Biletbayev in 1997: It very, very excite match – over 14 peoples was gather around the table – and then the game begin: First he hit the ball to me, then I hit the ball to him, then he hit the ball to me, then I hit the ball to him, but he do not manage hit the ball back to me! The score 1 – 0 Borat!

Then I hit the ball to him, then he hit the ball to me, then I hit the ball to him. . . he nearly miss it . . . but manage to hit the ball back to me, then I hit the ball to him, then he hit the ball to me and then I miss the ball. Score 1 – 1. Then He hit the ball to me, then I hit the ball to him, then he hit the ball to me, then I hit the ball to him....he nearly miss it...but manage to hit the ball back to me, then I hit the ball to him, then he hit the ball to me and then I hit the ball to him, then he hit the ball to me, then I hit the ball to him, he hit the ball to me, I hit the ball to him, he miss the ball. Score is now 2-1. Then he hit the ball to me, I hit the ball to him, he hit the ball to me, he almost miss the ball, but he manage to hit it to me, then I hit the ball to him, then he hit the ball to me, then I miss the ball. The score is now 2 POINTS FOR BORAT and also 2 points for KORKI BILATBAYEV. Then I hit the ball to him, then he hit the ball to me, then h e hit the ball to me, no that a mistake, it was in fact me who hit the ball to him, then he hit the ball to me, then I miss the ball. This very bad news! The score is now 2 points for Borat, but 3 points for Korki Bilatbayev! Now it his turn for make service – he hit the ball to me, I hit **the ball to him, he h**it the ball to me, I hit the ball to him, he almost miss the ball, but do not and hit the ball to me, then I hit the ball to him and he miss the ball. Great success! **The score i**s NOW 3 POINTS TO BORAT AND ALSO 3 POINTS TO KORKI BILATBAYEV. THEN HE HIT THE BALL TO ME, THEN I HIT THE BALL TO HIM, THEN HE HIT THE BALL TO ME, THEN I HIT THE BALL TO HIM, THEN HE HIT

ПИНГПОН ГРi NG PONG

THE BALL TO Me and I miss the ball! This bad news because once more he is infront as the score is now 3 points to Borat, but 4 points to Korki Bilatbayev. Then again he hit the ball to me, then I hit the ball to him, then he hit the ball to me, then I hit the ball to him, then he almost miss the ball, but do not, then I hit the ball to him and this time he do miss the ball! Great success once more! The scores is now 4 point for Borat and also 4 point for Korki Bilatbayev. Then he hit the ball to me, then I hit the ball to him, then he hit the ball to me, then I hit the ball to him, then he miss the ball. Can you believing this!? I am once more in the front! The scores is now Borat 5 points, Korki Bilatbayev 4 points! Then he hit the ball to me, then I hit the ball to him, then he hit the ball to me, the I hit the ball to him, then he hit the ball to me – I almost misses it, but I do not misses it, but instead I hit the ball to him, then he hits the ball to me, then I hit the ball to him, then he hits the ball to me, then I miss the ball. The scores is now Borat 5 points and Korki Bilatbayev also 5 points. It now turn of Borat for service of the ball. I hit the ball to him, he hit the ball to me, I hit the ball to him, he hit the ball to me, I hit the ball to him, he hit the ball to me, I hit the ball to him, he miss the ball.

Great success! This mean that I win this point and the scores is now Borat 6 points, Korki Bilatbayev 5 points! Then I hit the ball to him, then he hit the ball to me, then I hit the ball to him, then he hit the ball to me, I almost misses the ball, but manage to hit it to him, then he hits the ball to me, then I hit the ball to him, then he hits the ball to me, then I hit the ball to him, then he misses the ball!!! Great success!! The scores is now Borat 7 points, Korki 5 points, which means I has a lead of 2 points! Then I hit the ball to him, he hits the ball to me, I hit the ball to him, he hits the ball to me, I hits the ball to him, he hits the ball to me, I hits the ball to him, he hits the ball to me, I misses the ball. The scores is now Borat 7 points, Korki Bilatbayev 6 points. Then I hit the ball to him, then he hits the ball to me, then I hit the ball to him, then he almost misses the ball, but he do not miss the ball but instead hits the ball to me, I almost misses the ball but I do not, instead I hits the ball to him, then he hits the ball to me, then I hits the ball to him then he hits the ball to me, then I misses the ball. This very bad news because from earlier being leader, now I am no longer leader because the scores is Borat 7 points, Korki Bilatbayev also 7 points. Then I hit the ball to him, then he hit the ball to me, then I hit the ball to him, then he hit the ball to me, then I miss the ball. This very unpleased to me because it mean that now the scores is Borat 7 points and Korki Bilatbayev 8 points. It now turn of Korki Bilatbayev to do a serve the ball. He hit the ball to me – immediate I almost misses the ball!! But I do not and instead I hit the ball to him, then he hits the ball to me, then I hit the ball to him, then he hits the ball to me, then I hit the ball to him, then he almost misses the ball but instead he hits the ball to me, then I miss the ball! I cannot believing this – previous I was leadings by margin 2 point, but now instead I am losing by deficit of 2 points because the scores is now Borat 7 points and Korki Bilatbayev 9 points! Then he hit the ball to me, then I hit the ball to him, then he hit the ball to me, then I hit the ball to him, then he miss the ball! This good because now the scores is **Borat 8 points and Korki Bilatbayev 9 points meaning that deficit now reduce to one points. Then he hit the ball to me, then I hit the ball to him, then he hit the ball to me, then I miss the ball. This very disappoint to me because deficit once more 2 points because the score is now Borat 8 points and Korki Bilatbayev 10 points. Then he hit the ball to me, then I hit the ball to him, then he hit the ball to me, then I hit the ball to him, then he almost miss the ball, but do not and instead he hit the ball to me, then I** hit the ball to him, then again he almost miss the ball, but instead he hit the ball to me, then I hit the ball to him, then he miss the ball and I have score a point! The scores is now Borat 9 points and Korki Bilatbayev 10 points. Then he hit the ball to me, then I hit the ball to him, then he hits the ball to me, then I hits the ball to him, then he hits the ball to me, then I almost miss the ball but instead I hit the ball to him, then he hits the ball to me and I miss the ball! Can you again believings this how is it possible!? Once more deficit in scores is expand to two points because the scores is now **BORAT 9 POINTS AND KORKI BILATBAYEV 11 POINTS**. It now once again turn of Borat to do a service so I take the ball and I hit the ball to him, than he hit the ball to me, then I hit the ball to him, then he hits the ball to me, then I hit the ball to him, then he misses the ball!! Once again I have reduce trailings to one point and the scores is Borat 10 points and Korki Bilatbayev 11 points! Then I hit the ball to him, then he hit the ball to me, then I hit the ball to him, then he hit the ball to me, then I almost miss the ball but I do not, then I hit the ball to him, he almost misses the ball, but he do not and instead he hits the ball to me and I miss the ball. I cannot believe that once more it is possible for this to happening but it actual have and deficit have again become 2 points! Scores now is Borat 10 points and Korki Bilatbayev 12 points. Then I hit the ball to him, then he hits the ball to me, then I hit the ball to him, then he hits the ball to me, then I hit the ball to him and – great success – he misses the ball. I have win a point and the scores is now Borat 11 points and Korki Bilatbayev 12 points. Then I hit the ball to him, then he hit the ball to me, then I hit the ball to him, then he try hit the ball to me, but he miss the ball!!! WAWAWEEWA! I now evenstevens! Scores now is Borat 12 points and Korki Bilatbayev also 12 points! Then I hits the ball to him, then he hits the ball to me, then I hit the ball to him, then he hit the ball to me, then I hit the ball to him, then he hit the ball to me, then I hit the ball to him, then he hit the ball to me, then I hit the ball to him, then he almost miss the ball but do not and instead he hit the ball to me, then I miss the ball. This mean from previous being happy that I was level point score to him, now I not so happy as once again he is in a lead because the scores is now Borat 12 points and Korki Bilatbayev 13 points. It now turn once again of Korki Bilatbayev to do the service. He hit the ball to me, then I hit the ball to him, then he hit the ball to me, then I hit the ball to him, then he miss the ball! Great success – I have eradicate once more the deficit in score and the scores is now Borat 13 points and Korki Bilatbayev also 13 point. Then he hit the ball to me, then I hit the ball to him, then he hit the ball to me, then I hit the ball to him and then he hit the ball to me and I miss the ball! Once again I am no longer on equal points to him but instead has one point less since the scores is now Borat 13 points and Korki Bilatbayev 14 points! This not the only bad news because the ball have also run across the floor and become lost under a pile of wood that is in corner of the room. Eventually it is found, but it have a small dents in it which is remove by place the ball in a bowl of water that is hot, but not boiling. Then he hit the ball to me, then I hit the ball to him, then he hit the ball to me, then I hit the ball to him, then he hit the ball to me, then I hit the ball to him, then he hit the ball to me, then I hit the ball to him, then he hit the ball to me, then I hit the ball to him, then he hit the ball to me, then I hit the ball to him, then he hit the ball to me, then I hit the ball to him, then he hit the ball to me, then I hit the ball to him, then he miss the ball! This very please to me, since now this mean the score is now Borat 14 points and Korki Bilatbayev also 14 points! Then he hit the ball to me, then I hit the ball to him, then he hit the ball to me, then I hit the ball to him, then he hit the ball to me, then I hit the ball to him, then he hit the ball to me, then I hit the ball to him, then he hit the ball to me, then I hit the ball to him, then he hit the ball to me, then he almost miss the ball, but do not and instead he hit the ball to me, then I hit the ball to him, then he hit the ball to me, then I hit the ball to him, then he hit the ball to me, then I hit the ball to him, then he hit the ball to me, then I hit the ball to him, then he hit the ball to me, then I hit the ball to him, then he hit the ball to me, then – can you believing this? I miss the ball one more times!! The scores is now Borat 14 points and Korki Bilatbayev 15 points! Then he hit the ball to me, then I hit the ball to him, then he hit the ball to me, then he hit the ball to me, then – he almost miss the ball but do not and instead he hit the ball to me and then it is me who miss the ball which disaster since it meaning the scores is now Borat 14 points and Korki Bilatbayev 16 points! I has now again a deficit of points of two points! It now once more turn of Borat to do a service, so I hit the ball to him, then he hit the ball to me, then I hit the ball to him, then he hit the ball to me, then I hit the ball to him, then he hit the ball to me, then he almost miss the ball, but do not and instead he hit the ball to me, then I hit the ball to him, then he hit the ball to me, then I hit the ball to him, then he hit the ball to me, then I hit the ball to him, then he hit the ball to me, then I hit the ball to him, then he hit the ball to me, then I hit the ball to him and he miss the ball! Great success! Consequence of this is that deficit reduce to one points and the scores is Borat 15 points and Korki Bilatbayev 16 points. Then I hit the ball to him then he hit the ball to me, then I hit the ball to him, then he hit the ball to me, then I almost misses the ball, but I do not and instead I hit the ball to him, then he almost miss the ball but do not and instead he hit the ball to me and the n I miss the ball. Once more I am in arrears of score of him by margin two points since the score is now Borat 15 points and Korki Bilatbayev 17 points! Then I hit the ball to him, then he hit the ball to me, then I hit the ball to him, then he hit the ball to me, then he hit the ball to me then he miss the ball!! The point is won by Borat!! Deficit have been reduction to one point again and the scores is Borat 16 points and Korki Bilatbayev 17 points! Then I hit the ball to him and immediate once more he miss the ball!! It true! He do not hit the ball and I have win another point which mean we is again evenstevens and the scores is Borat 17 points and Korki Bilatbayev 17 points!! Then I hit the ball to him, then he hit the ball to me, then I hit the ball to him, then he hit the ball to me, then I hit the ball to him, then he hit the ball to me, then I hit the ball to him, then he hit the ball to me, then I hit the ball to him, then he hit the ball to me, then I hit the ball to him, then he hit the ball to me, then I hit the ball to him, then he hit the ball to me, then he almost miss the ball, but do not and instead he hit the ball to me, then I hit the ball to him, then he hit the ball to me, then I hit the ball to him, then he hit the ball to me, then I hit the ball to him, then he almost miss the ball but do not and instead he hit the ball to me, then I hit the ball to him and this time he do miss the ball! I am now in lead of the game by margin of one point! I so excite! The scores is now Borat 18 points and Korki Bilatbayev 17 points! It once again turn of Korki Bilatbayev to do a service so he hit the ball to me, then I hit the ball to him, then he hit the ball to me, then I hit the ball to him, then he hit the ball to me, then I miss the ball! I cannot believe this! From previous being one point in lead I have lose a point which means we is level points since the score is now Borat 18 points and Korki Bilatbayev also 18 points. Then he hit the ball to me, then I hit the ball to him, then he hit the ball to me, then I hit the ball to him, then he miss the ball!! It true – once again he have miss the ball with result I win the point and the scores is now Borat 19 points and Korki Bilatbayev 18 points. Then he hit the ball to me, then I hit the ball to him, then he hit the ball to me, Then almost miss the ball, but do not and instead he hit the ball to me, then I hit the ball to him, then he hit the ball to me, then I hit the ball to him, then he hit the ball to me, then I hit the ball to him, then he almost miss the ball but do not and instead he hit the ball to me, then I hit the ball to him and he miss the ball! Wawaweewa! I have win another points with result that I now need only win one further point to have secure victory of entire game. What will happen next? He hit the ball to me, then I hit the ball to him, then he hit the ball to me, then I hit the ball to him, then he miss the ball!!! The game is over since I have win that point! Final score is 21 point Borat, and 18 point Korki Bilatbayev. Borat is viktor!

ХОББИА

· SUNBATHE

I am very much enjoy sunbathes my body.

Here I am relax on beach at Astana Funworld Family Resort.

For protection against sunburning I make rub squirrel cheese on my skins

ХОББИА

· **SUSPEND OF WEIGHTS FROM TESTES SATCHEL**

Another hobby that I very goods at is suspending heavy weights from my testes satchel. National record holder is Premier Nazarbamshev, who manage lift gearbox of tractor for

7.1 seconds! You don't believe me, you must see him do it at the opening of parliament every year.

My personal record car battery, which I suspend for 4.6 second!

91

ДРУГИЕ ЧЛЕНЫ СЕМЬИ

• OTHER FAMILY MEMBERS

In additions to myself, I have **one** brother and two sister.

BILO

My brother name is Bilo – he is retard with 204 teeth (197 in mouth, 7 in nose). He have small head like a chicken, but very strong arms.

Bilo also live in village of Kuczek. He have a beautiful cage where all day long he look on porno and rub, rub, rub. He is sex crazy!

One time my brother Bilo make a sexytime with Lilya Tulyakbay (she daughter of my mother and my neighbour Nursultan Tulyakbay – he still asshole), with result birth a very strange one who is now perform in State Circus. Great success!

This Bilak – he 13, but still have no moustache!

• MY CHILDRENS

I has three childrens – Bilak, Biram and Hooeylewis.

BILAK AND BIRAM

Bilak have age now 13 years and is my least favourite son.

Bilak have identical tWIN BROTher. His name Biram and he also 13 year of age.

Same as me, Biram have career in industry televiski – he actor in Kazakh children': programme 'TeleVISKistomatches'. He was very nervous when he first appear on cameras – especial for the sex scenes.

92

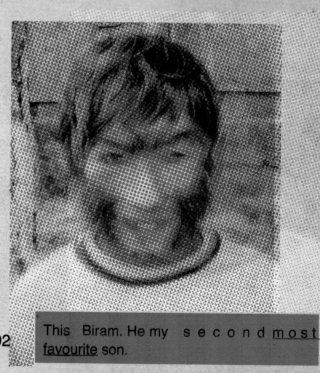

This Biram. He my second most favourite son.

This wife of Bilak. I do not know her name

My son Bilak have a WIFE and they have recent been celebrate the most joyfuls and happiest day of their lives – the birth of their first child a beautiful, happyface, healthy boy, who is for sale.

PLEASE western moviestars Madonnas and Angelica Jollie – if you are read this, consider make purchase this baby – it Kazakh child and so do not require much food and will be strong enough for work in field or factory within 4 year. Also, if you do not like colour, I can paint it However you wish – chocolate face, yellow, Red Indian, anything you like. I can even glue fur on it if you prefer? Price just 1 0 0 U S D o l l a r – I sure this much more cheap than you payings for your Africans.

TELEVISKI-STOMACHES! FAVOURITE FOR ALL CHILDRENS OF KAZAKSTAN!

These is not real creatures – there is people inside. My son Biram the second from left with porno movie on his stomatch.

93

СУПРУ ГИ
• WIVES

I have been marry three occasion. My first wife name was name Ludmilla – I buy her when she 12 for 15 litre of insecticide – at time I think this bargain, but it end up she not worth it. My second wife was name Oxana. Like Ludmilla, she start good – her vagine was tight like a man's anoos and she would use her great strength to pull a large Krinski plough for many hours without food or rest. But after few year, she too become difficult – she very angry all time and when I instruct her to use her muscles to work in fields, she would instead use her great power to make a rape on me maybe 8 or 9 times every day. Oxana now also dead – when I in America, she was attack, violate and break by a bear while she was walk my brother Bilo in the woods. Two week later the bear that do this was caught and appear before Kuczek Magistrates who give it maximum sentence for murder of woman – public shavings of it fur.

This Oxana's funeral.

This my new wife Luenell – she make most delicious tit cheese

94

Ludmilla now dead. I remember very clear the day this happen – at time, I was get mouth party from A prostitute when I receive message from my neighbour Nursultan Tuly akBay, that he had shoot a very large bear. I immediate leave my sister and return home, where I was

very angry to find out he had actually shoot my wife. This made me very in a temper, because I was look forward to eat bear meat that night.

This Ludmilla while she still beautiful. It did not last long.

Here Ludmilla is wear her red dress. When she die it was give to my second wife, Oxana – and when she die, it was give to my current wife, Luenell.

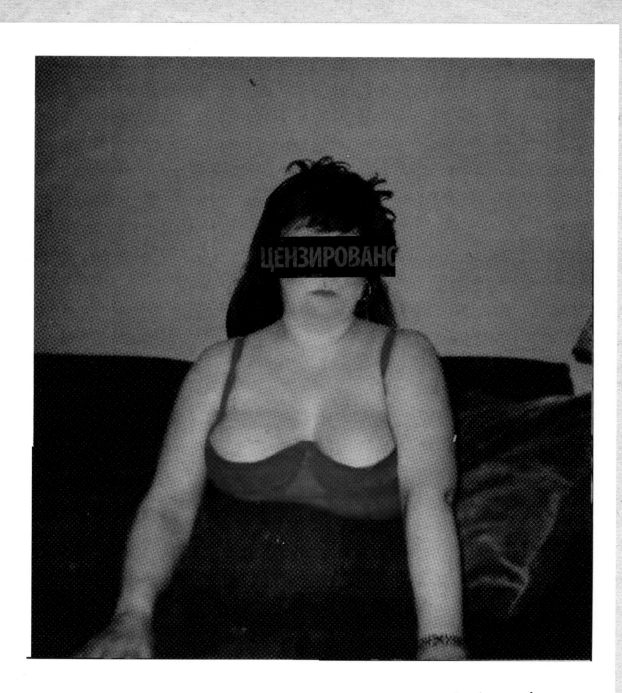

In this picture, my   dead wife Ludmilla have had her face cover   by decree of
Kazakh Censor, who   decide it was too offensive for people to look on.

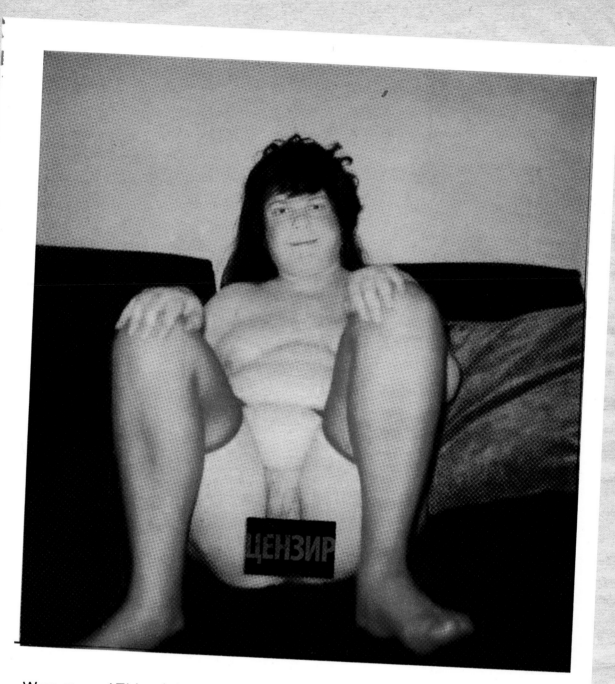

Wawaweewa! This picture was send to me while I was working in US and A and was feelings lonely. It was the very first photograph ever taken by my son Bilak.

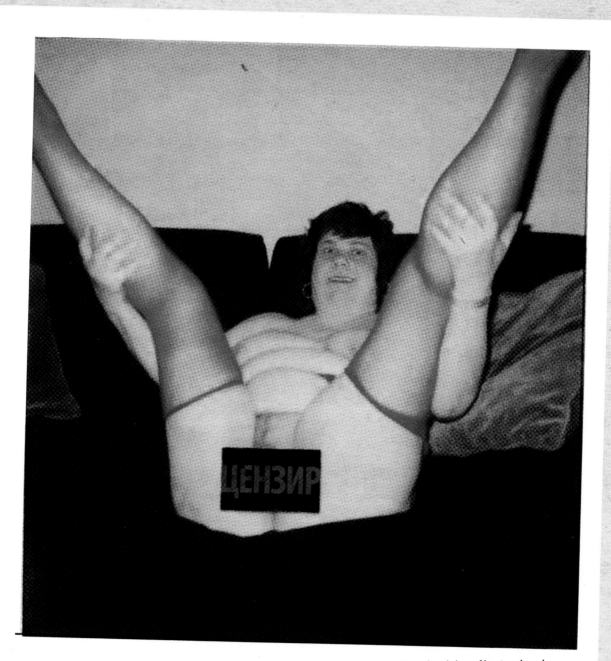

This the second picture ever taken by my so**n** **B**ilak and it win him first prize in his school photographys competition.

cЕСТРЫ

• SISTERS
NATALYA AND RAUMILYA

In addition my brother Bilo, I has two sister – name Natalya and Raumilya. One of them prostitute, the other is teacher. This obvious bring great shame on my family, but no matter how much we persuade my sister Raumilya, she will not sell her body for sexytime.

Natalya used to be number 4 prostitute in all of Kazakhstan, but has recent slip to number 6. She was very disappoint about this news but was please to be recent receive award from ALMATY Chamber of Commerce for Best Sex In Mouth.

This my sister Raumilya. She 5 months younger than me.

This Raumilya when she win 3rd prize in Miss Kazakhstan contest. **1**st prize was win by Karylgash Atmekova, but some people say she had cheat by attach rocks to her teets to make them dangle extra long.

My sister Raumilya and I used to have much funtime together — here
we are play game where we pretend to be husband and wife!   You should
try with your sister — it nice!

Raumilya die shortly after this picture was take when my brother Bilo also try to play the husband and wife game with her and accidentally break her.

МОИ ДЕТИ

• HOOEY LEWIS

My favourite son have age 18 and is name Hooeylewis. He do not yet have any
wives and I am very concern that he may be homosexual.

This Hooeylewis. He name after sexy American popstar Hooeylewis.

Hooeylewis mother Ludmilla die when he was 12 year old, which mean for food, he then had to suck on his sister's teets.

Hooeylewis is a very talent actor — here he is pretend to be a man with a big ears!

One day, as eldest son, Hooeylewis will inherit the chair of my family. In the meantimes, when we watch pornos together, he must sit on the floors.

Hooeylewis very strong! After this photograph was taken, he carry me like this all the way from my house to the village kindergarten.

Hooeylewis very big for his age and I hope that one day he may reach size necessary to qualify to be candidate for Government Minister! Great success!

The Kazakh Ministry of Information would like to recognize the minor assistance of the following westerners in the production of this journal . . .

Jon Butler, Peter Gethers, Tony Lyons, Rebecca Holland, Michael Collica, Nicola Plumb, Tony McSweeney, Suzanne Herz, Stephen Rubin, Michael Palgon, Janet Cooke, Kim Cacho, Deborah Bull, Alison Rich, John Pitts, Kris Fogel, Monica Levinson, Jason Alper, Thomas Kolavek, Robyn Wholey, Brian Lipson, Johnny Geller, Dan Strone, Ben Eagle, Alex Hilhorst, Wendy Kirk

Photo Credits: Cover, Kazhak side, clockwise from left: Ruben Fleisher; "BORAT: CULTURAL LEARNINGS OF AMERICA FOR MAKE BENEFIT GLORIOUS NATION OF KAZAKHSTAN" © 2006 Twentieth Century Fox, all rights reserved; Ruben Fleisher; Mel Gibson statue: Statue: © Authors Image/Alamy; Mel Gibson: Getty Images; Village: ©Michel Setboun/Sygma/Corbis Cover, US and A side, clockwise from left: Ruben Fleisher; Robyn Wholey; "BORAT: CULTURAL LEARN-INGS OF AMERICA FOR MAKE BENEFIT GLORIOUS NATION OF KAZAKHSTAN" © 2006 Twentieth Century Fox, all rights reserved; Jason Alper; Ruben Fleisher
Touristic Guidings to Kazakhstan: p. 27, top, © Reuters/Corbis; p. 27, #2, Paul Harris/Getty Images; p. 27, bottom right, Carl & Ann Purcell/Corbis; p 53: Horse on book cover, Colin Monteath/Hedgehog House/Getty Images; p. 55, Tony Waltham/Getty Images; p. 59, Statue: © Authors Image/Alamy; p. 59, Mel Gibson: Getty Images; p. 59, Village: ©Michel Setboun/Sygma/Corbis; p. 61, TV, Jupiter Images; p. 61, Roller coaster, ClassicStock; p. 62, Panda, Xinhua/XINHUA/Corbis; p. 62, Pig and Ground, Johner/Getty Images; p. 75, Rocket only, MAXIM MARMUR/AFP/Getty Images; p. 80, © Arthur Rothstein/Corbis.
Grateful acknowledgement is also given to the following for the Kazakh side: "BORAT: CULTURAL LEARNINGS OF AMERICA FOR MAKE BENEFIT GLO-RIOUS NATION OF KAZAKHSTAN" © 2006 Twentieth Century Fox, All rights reserved (pp. 17, 20, 69, 76, 79, 87, 93, 104-109); Ant Hines (pp. 18, 30-both at bottom, 36, 54, 56, 57, 78, 79, 90, 92-both, 94-bottom; Robyn Wholey (pp. 27-bottom, #3, 82, 83, 86-bottom left, Jason Alper (pp. 5, 30 top left, 84-bottom, 85); Ruben Fleisher (pp 34, 67, 86-right, 91, 94-top); J. Christian Walsh (pp. 5, 84-top, both); Special Thanks to Talkback Productions and Channel Four Television for photographs from the series "Da Ali G Show" (pp. 95-99); photographs from the series "Da Ali G Show," courtesy of Home Box Office, Inc. (pp. 100-103); mOcean (pp. 29, 33, 39-44, 47, 49, 73); the song entitled "In My Country There Is Problem" from the series "Da Ali G Show," courtesy of Home Box Office, Inc.
Touristic Guidings to US and A: p. 12, left, © Pascal Baril/Kipa/Corbis; p. 12, right, © Richard Carson/Reuters/Corbis; p. 13, top right, AFP/AFP/Getty Images; p. 13, bottom left, TIM SLOAN/AFP/Getty Images; p. 17, top right, © Bob Krist/Corbis; p. 18, © Corbis; pp. 20-21, © Gavin Bond/Corbis Outline; p. 38, bottom left: © STR/epa/Corbis; p. 44, top right, Raimund Koch/Getty Images; p. 46, top, © James Leynse/Corbis; p. 50, Grady Coppell/Getty Images; p. 52, both, © Joshua Roberts/Reuters/Corbis; p. 61, top, © Charles E. Rotkin/Corbis; p. 61, bottom, © Martin Philbey/ZUMA/Corbis; p. 62, © Jonathan Blair/Corbis; p. 63, top right, © Bettmann/Corbis; p. 63, left, © CARDINALE STEPHANE/Corbis Sygma; p. 63, bottom right, © Rune Hellestad/Corbis.
Grateful acknowledgment is also given to the following for US and A side: "BORAT: CULTURAL LEARNINGS OF AMERICA FOR MAKE BENEFIT GLORI-OUS NATION OF KAZAKHSTAN" © 2006 Twentieth Century Fox, all rights reserved; David Bernstein (p. 17-bottom); Alexandra Lambrinidis (pp 40, 64, 65); Ant Hines (p. 33, top right, p. 41); Jason Alper (pp. 3, 11, 16, 26-both, 28, 42, 49, 56-both); Kris Fogel (pp. 27, 33-left, 38-top); Peter Baynham (p. 51); Robyn Wholey (p. 45); Ruben Fleisher (pp. 5, 14, 19, 22-25, 29-31, 34, 36, 39, 47, 48, 54, 55, 58-59, 66, 67); Todd Schulman (p. 6, 57, 60)

йечатания введения для иектора гбъема – исА и А

• INTRODUCTION TYPINGS FOR SECTOR OF VOLUME – US AND A

Jagshemash peoples of Kazakhstan – 'howdy pardners' peoples of western nations – my name Borat Sagdiyev I would like make congratulate you for acquisitions this Volume of literatures I have author – I am certains it will prove a most excellent source of information for both tourists and scholars* and also provide nice material for make hand relief.

This sector of volume is dedicate to informations useful for peoples traveling to minor nation of US and A and is guarantee to contain only facts, since the writings come only from personal experience of Borat Sagdiyev, or from extensive archive of Kazakh Ministry of Propaganda.

Inspirations to make publish a touristic guidings book to minor nation US and A have origins in a most epic voyage I make to this country two years past to film documentary for the Kazakh Ministry Of Information.

The resulting moviefilm (entitle "Borat: Cultural Learnings Of America For Make Benefit Glorious Nation Of Kazakhstan"), was subsequent released by America's Capitalist Fox Corporation, who honoured in full the contract they had made with the Kazakh Government. This result in windfall for my country of nearly 300 US Dollar and 2,500 electronic clock radios Great success! I am hope this volume literature brings my country similar riches.

Chenquieh;
Borat Sagdiyev

* Warnings! Be most careful to not leave this book in place where it can be found by a small child – or even worse, a woman. You will recall the story of Karylgash Utmanalybev – "the woman who read a book" Her female brain was not sufficient powerful for such a thing and she became crazy inside head and killed her husband with her own leg chains and choke to death while eating her own shoe. If your wife start to read she will too have crazy thoughts. She will start moaning and saying "Borat I do not want to pull plough, Borat I don't want to dig hole, Borat, I pregnant, tractor tyre too heavy to carry" You have been warn.

Этот гид произведён Казахстанским Министерством туризма и Досугом и обеспечен авторское право вышеупомянутой организацией, так не берите гребаную мочу. ©2007

ГЛАВА 1

SECTOR OF VOLUME

HISTORY, GEOGRAPHIES AND SYSTEM POLITIK OF US and A

MAP OF US and A •

FASCINATING FACTS ON •
NATION US and A

SYSTEM POLITIK OF US •
and A

M C K · G CMY S1 M C S2 G S11 S

MAP OF U.S.&A.

KEY TO MAPS

MINEFIELD	
JEWS (ATTENTION! NO FENCES!)	
COWBOYS	
REDINDIANS	
TELEPHONE	
CHOCOLATE FACES	
HOMOSEXUALS	
PLACE FOR CHILDRENS PLAYING	
MACHINE THAT RELEASE WATER FOR DRINK	
LAVOLATORY FOR MAKE A SHIT	
SWIMMINGS POOL	
MICDONODLDS RESTAURANTS	
PROSTITUTES	

ALABAMA

LOS ANGELES

LOS VEGA

DISNEYS LAND

CALIFORNIAS

SAN FRANCISO

PACIFIC LIFE OCEAN

ALASKAS (LEPER COLONY)

HAWAI

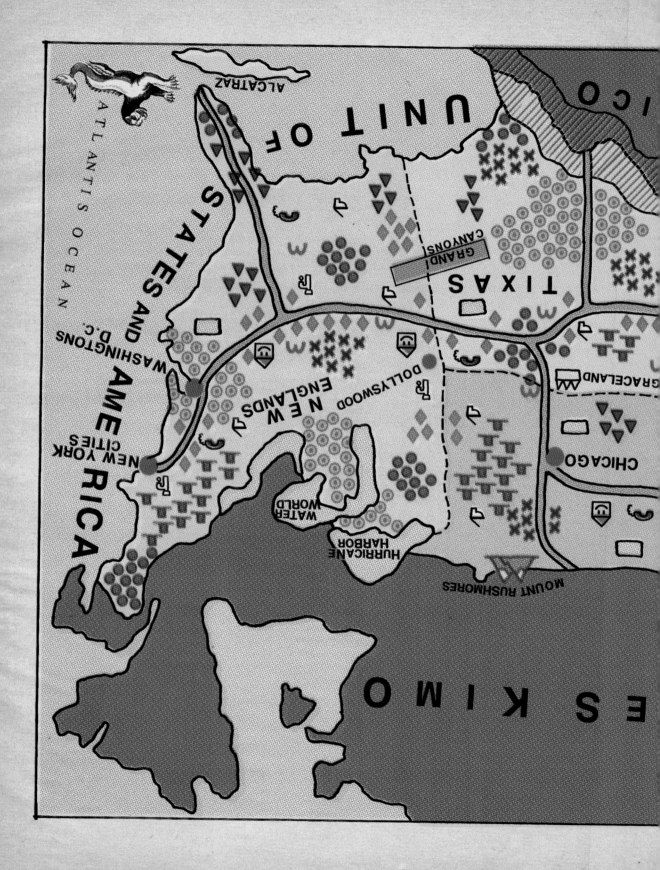

Ћстория, География и иистема, йолитическая из исА и А

HISTORY, GEOGRAPHIES AND SYSTEM POLITIK OF US AND A

US and A is a minor capitalist nation locate in northern hemisector of the globe, 15,000 days walk to the west of Kazakhstan. Discovered by the great Kazakh explorer Yiltan Yuranambev in year 1825, it have a very nice geographys, with mountains, desert and great fertile plains with excellent agricultures.

HERE IS SOME MORE FASCINATINGS FACT ON NATION US AND A ...

- Wealth of US and A is a staggerings, it have a gross domestic products of 13 trillion dollars – this equivalent to almost 27,000,000,000,000,000,000, 000,000,000,000,000,000,000,000,000,000,000,000,000,000,000,000,000,00 0,000,000,000,000,000 billion Kazakh Tenge !

- Principal exports of US and A is DVD pornos and televiskis programmes - my favourite is name 'Dallas'. In two week time in Kazakhstan, we will find out who it was who shoot JRs! I think it was Sue Helen.

- US and A is a nuclear power and have so far conduct tests of atomic bombs by explode them on Pacific islands of Bikini Atoll, Christmas Island and Japan – all with great success! They now ready to be use in anger if it ever necessary.

- America has very advance space programme. After Kazakhstan, it was the second nation to place a man on the moon.

- Although US and A is very strict with laws and orders, it have most humane method of execution in the world – lethal injections. Kazakhstan recent adopt this method also and we now finish our criminals by pumping 7 gallons of battery acid into their anoos.

- Most peoples of US and A follows a religion name 'christianitys', which makes worship of a man name Jesus Christs. I think he probably Kazakh, since he was born in a shed with pigs and cows and his mother did not know who had make her pregnants.

US and A have excellent agricultures. Their fruits is most delicious you will ever taste.

ПОЛИТИКА СИСТЕМЫ США И A

• SYSTEM POLITIK OF US AND A

Politik of US and A is very liberal and ANY citizen can become Premier, no matter what their backgrounds - in the last 40 year, a criminal, a retard and a sex-offender have all had this job. To get change of leader, there is on average a coup every 4 year. Current Premier is Mighty Warlord, George Walter Bush

This current Premier of US and A – George Walter Bush

This his father, Barbara, who was Premier before him

USEFUL KNOWLEDGES ON AMERICAN SYSTEM POLITIK...

• Although there is one Supreme Leader, US and A is split into fifty separate States (the smallest is Alabama, the biggest is Waterworld) and each one is ruled by its own Warlord. Most powerful is leader of Californias, **Arnold The Barbarian**

• Everyone in US and A can vote, including Chocolate Faces, although their votes is not actually counted.

This Arnold celebrating victory in battle to be Governor of California in 2003. I do not know where his chram and testes are? Perhaps he is play the game wnere you place them between your legs and pretend to be a girl?

Hillary Clintons is hopes to be Premier again in 2008. Here she is with a basketball player.

ГЛАВА 2

SECTOR OF VOLUME

2

THE PEOPLES OF US and A

COWBOYS •
REDINDIANs •
CHocoLATE FACEs•
AMERICAN WOMEnS •
LOOleE LooLEES •
THE JEW•

ЋЮДИ ИСА И А
• THE PEOPLES OF US AND A

When you travellings to US and A, you will notice many, many things that is different to Kazakhstan, for examples, EVERY town has electricity - and for more than two hours a day! Dogs in US and A is used for companion. It ridiculous! In Kazakhstan, they are for use as garnish for horse dish, for sexytime and to clean a man's anoos with tongue, And it true, Americans has riches beyond your wildest dreams – with some families eatings a Micdonalds Hamboorger every single month! But biggest differences of all that you will see is the peoples who lives in US and A – they are strange! There is three type of them, Redindians, Chocolate Faces and Cowboys (also, there is jew, homosexual and woman, but I will dealing with these separate).

• COWBOYS

In Kazakhstan, 'cowboy' is name give to a child with nuclear retardation who is born with black and white fur on his body and six tit on his stomatche. In US and A, Cowboys (also known as 'Vanilla Faces') is most common of all Americans tribes.

Here I am dress as American Cowboy for time when I sing at a rodeo. This is type of circus where a man try to take a horses virgin for the first time.

HERE SOME FASCINATINGS FACT ABOUT COWBOY

• Most commons names of Cowboys is Trevor, Geoffrey and Phillip

• Cowboys lives all across US and A, but highest concentrations is in Dodge City, Redneck and San Franciscos

• Some of famous cowboys includes Mighty Warlord George Walter Bush, Hero Johnwayne and Madonna

From my observations, cowboys has phenis size average 15.4 centimetre. Here is some photograph I have take of them making urines.

Cowboys is real men, very dangerous

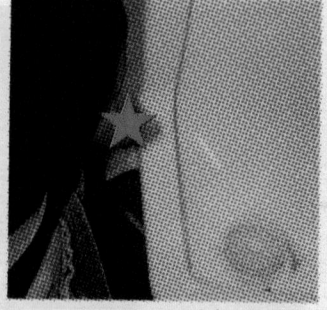 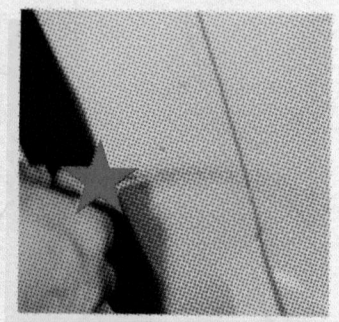

This man would not tell me his name.

This man would not tell me his name either.

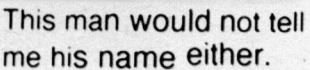

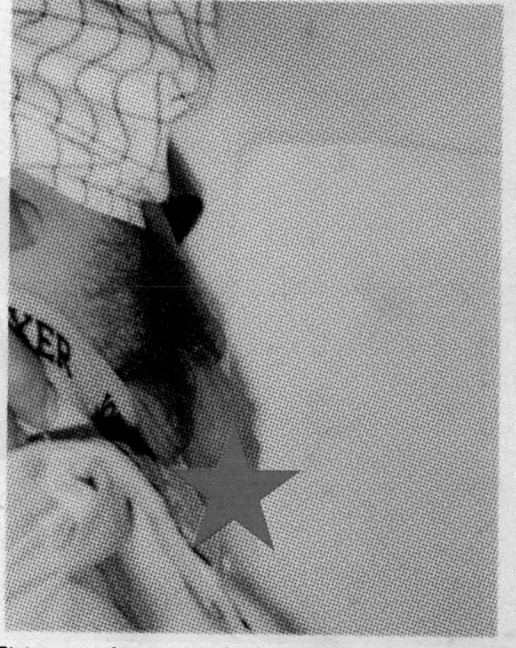

For discover more about cowboys, I would suggesting that you look on the moviefilm, Brokeback Mountains. I have hear rumourings that it have undercurrents homosexual nature, but I think this just anti-west communist propagandas. I have see it many many time and I see no evidence that the two men who put their chrams in each other's anoos is just strong friends

This man's name is Laurence. He was very friendly – he invite me back his house where he give me massage and we have Jacuzzi. It was nice!

• REDINDIANS

Redindians is second most usual peoples to see in US and A. They lives in a special type of pointed tent, called a casino. For many year people have say they are a bad peoples who attacks vanilla faces for no reason – but I think they are nice!* This is what typical Redindian is look like! For many year, you could go to US and A and have a very much funtime shooting these Redindians, but I recent discover that it now illegal. I would, once again, like to take this opportunity to apologize to the staff of the Potatwatomi Casino in Kansas. I did not know! There was no sign!

Redindian of year 2007. This man will probably have between 15 and 20 wife.

HERE IS SOME MOST INTERESTINGS FACT ON THESE REDINDIAN

• Do not believe reports that Red Indians do not perform 'scalping' anymore. I met a Red Indian in a bar 'Hank's Place' in New York and when he removed his trousers in the bathroom, I notice that his pussyfur had been scalped.

• Favourite drink of Redindians is delicious fruit cordial name Mountain Dew.

• Most common names of Redindians is Sitting Michael and Running William.

• Famous Redindians includes Mowgli, John Rambo and Apu.

• Redindians lives in tribes – the most common is Commanches, Apache and Wu Tang Clang.

• CHOCOLATE FACES

As everybody knows, Kazakhstan have for many year now had community of people with chocolate colour skin – his name Gogol The Clown and everybody love him. He live in Almaty and sometime appear in Kazakh State Circus where the childrens like to marvel at his appearance and touch his magical hair. Can you imagine my surprisings when I arrive in US and A and discover that there is over 1000 peoples here just like Gogol! My friend Azamat joked that America is like William Wonka's Chocolate Face Manufacturing Plant! And good news is, just like Gogol The Clown, they is also very nice and very friendly – infacts, they my favorite Americans people!

---

* Please ignore this remarks. Since first writings of these Redindians, I have hear some very sad news. My friend Viktor Hotelier tell me that he see on television that Hero Johnwayne was attack by Redindians, who shoot him with arrows and that he now dead.

If you also want look on this Chocolate Face man, I see him in Los Angeles, Californias, near to the gasoline shop named Exxon

HERE IS SOME USEFUL FACT ON CHOCOLATE FACE AMERICANS

• Young Chocolate Face mens 'hangs out' in groups that is call 'pussys'. Not anyone can join – one time I ask a young Chocolate Face if I could have entry to his pussy and he was a very angry and tell me 'NO!'

• DO NOT attempt make purchase of a Chocolate Face American – this was make illegal in 1987

• For relaxation times, Chocolate Face Americans likes to make popular music with instrument name 'banjo'.

• Famous American Chocolate Faces includes Edward Murphy, Lionel Ritchies, Alan Jolsons, Banjoman Louis Armstrong and the Fresh Princes of Bellairs

• Chocolate Face Americans lives all across the US and A, although best place for go to and look on them is Sesame Street in New York City

• Most popular name of Chocolate face community is Colin

• Chocolate Face Americans hates going on aeroplanes

• Chocolate Faces very much like discodancing. Their favourite dancing is name 'The Robots'

• They has chocolate colour over entire body – not just hands and face

Here I am dress as five typical American mens

• AMERICAN WOMENS

If there is one things that everyone already knows about US and A, it is that it home to the most beauitul womens in the word – Pamela CJ Andersons, Liza Minelli, Elizabeth Taylors, Courtney Loves, Dakota Fanning, …the listings is endless. But these ladies will not just have a sexytime with any man they have just met (possible exception Courtney Loves) and it not possible to offer their fathers 15 litres of insecticide in exchange for them - in America, in order to gain entry to a lady vagine, you must first do a ritual name 'datings'.

I did not discover where this little girl lives, since she remained in the urines cubicle for over 4 hours and it become too boring waitings for her emerge

Yogas class in US and A is very good place for meet pretty ladies.

It do not matter what you do, they do not run away.

• DATINGS

This is formal procedure that you must follow if you want American wife. It very similar to prostitution, except instead of give a woman money directly for sexytime, you must use the same money to buy her food and presents and when you have reach the right amount she will grant you sexytime.

It is considered very bad manners in US and A if you do not make you face and hair look nice before forcing yourself on a ladies.

If you are in Los Angeles and do not have a camera, but still wish to see a lady minoos clothes for make a hand relief, then I recommend look on this apartment. It at the junction of 1st Streets and Robinson Streets, address Apt #324, Hamerton Court. The lady who live in there usual appears in just her antipants between hours 6 am and 8:30 am on days Monday to Thursday. She usual do not appear on Fridays mornings because she stay in another place on Thursdays nights – I do not know where, I have try to follow her to discover, but she have a fast motorcar. Best place for spy on her apartment is from behind garbage bins of Mexican restaurant opposites, which is also very useful if you are stay for several hours, because these bins is contain many delicious snackings!

• AMERICAN PROSTITUTES

If you are unwilling to spending the time it take to do a datings, America has some very nice prostitutes – but most of them very expensive! For price of a hand-party in US and A, in Kazakhstan you could make entry to Premier Nazarbamshev's wife....in small hole!

If you are looking also for a beautiful lady just like this one in photograph, I met her in a bar of New York City called 'The Cock Ring'. One time I go there and I was very lucky, because there were 50 mens in the club and only one woman – and who did she choose? The woman choose me - ladies like Borat! She remind me very much of a Kazakh woman - she had a beautiful long hair, much hair on arms, and some on face, and a voice deeper than mine. I invite her my hotel room. She give me a drink and I must been very tired because I cannot remember what happened after. The next morning, she had disappear and my anoos was hang loose like mouth of tired dog. I cannot explaining why!?

There is some bargains though – for just 10 US Dollar I receive a most excellent mouth-party from this beautiful lady.

• AMERICAN PORNOGRAPHY

If you are on extreme tight budgets and do not wish spending money on prostitutes, there is much excellent pornographys in US and A for make a handparty. Alternative to purchase pornographys, in US and A, there is many opportunity for generate you own sexy photos.

I have calculate that best time to photograph a girl minoos most clothing is 1 minute and 17 seconds after she have enter changings cubicle

Here I am hide behind a plants pot from a gypsy who has shrunk me. No I am not! It is the plant pot that is big and I have not actual been shrunk! These pots is in Tixas and is a good place from which to launch ambush on any pretty ladies who walks past.

I discover that for some reason it forbid to make photographs of ladies in store name Abertcrombies and Fitchs. This very confusing as there is no sign to say so! All other place is legal.

ADVANTAGE OF WOMEN US AND A

- **Appearance** – compare to Kazakh womens, American ladies is very beautiful – they has more hair on head than body, their tits grows only on front not back also and they has teeth only on inside of their mouths

- **Sexytime** – America is one of the 7 greatest countries in the world. Not just because it have very powerful army, and mighty leaders, but also because it is inventor of 'position blowjob'. Since my return to Kazakhstan I have spread knowledge of this. It a very convenient way for achieve liquid explosion as there no need to remove wife from cage.

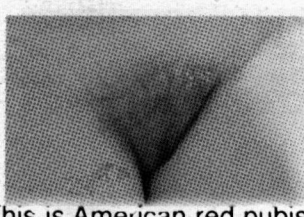

This is American red pubis. If you are lucky enough to find one, in Kazakhstan it worth more than diamonds.

- **Pubis** - very few american womens has pubis – they is trained to remove it themselves and do not need shepherd. I do not know what then happens to it, since I have not seen any for sale in American shops. It must all be export, unless it removed because of recent nuclear leak or infestation of Kratzouli? I have hear rumour that when it grows, some American ladies has pubis of yellow, or even red!

- **Retardation** – average occurrence of retardation in family for Kazakh woman is 59%. For American woman it 0.04% - which is problem if you is specific trying to breed strange ones for sell to the circus.

- **Weak body** – US and A ladies do not have a big muskles, this mean that whenever you need to, it easy to carry them against their will.

DISADVANTAGE OF WOMEN US AND A

- **Expensive** – to keep an American womans may take more money than for a horse! Many of them has been very spoiled and will be use to meals every single day and to sleep indoors at night. Also, because they has so little fur on their bodies it necessary spend more moneys on clothings them in Kazakh winter.

- **Permit to speak** – unlike in Kazakhstan, in America, there is no law preventing womens from speaking unless they are spoken to and consequent they will do a nag nag nag nag nag all the times. Very boring.

- **Weak vagines** – they would probably break if require to produce more than 18 sons in twelve year period.

- **Weak body** – US and A ladies do not have a big muskles, this mean that they will not be so good when require to pull plow

- **Tit Cheese** – Cheese made from milk of wife tit best part of a marriage! US and A ladies are too lazy to make this.

• AMERICAN LOOLEE LOOLEES (HOMOSEXUALS)

In addition to Cowboys, Chocolate Faces and Redindians, US and A has more homosexuals than any other country in world (apart of course from France). And just like in Kazakhstan after the Tulyakev Reforms, it very hard to spot them – they do not have to wear blue hats and even more confusings, some homosexuals in US and A has no moustache!

I cannot tell you for certains how to recognizing loolee-loolees in US and A, all I can do is telling what I have learn of them

• Many of them advertises their services in public lavolatories – if there is telephone number on a walls there from a man offering mouth-party for 5 dollar, then that man is probably homosexual (if his name Brett and his number is (466) 555-0306, then he is DEFINITELY a homosexual).

Can you believe it – these men is actual homosexuals despite their moustaches and strong muskles.

• It is legal for homosexuals in US and A to drive motorcars between hours of 4 pm and 7 pm. American Freeways has a special lane for them which is mark by a diamond shape. You will see them together in vehicles here, driving to edge of forest to make bang bang bang in anoos.

This is the motorcar that homosexuals drives in US and A.

• Homosexuals in US and A clean their teeths every single day with a small brush.

• Some famous homosexuals American men includes Spiderman, Ronald Micdonalds and Madonna.

• Most common names of homosexual in US and A is Marshall, Curtis and Sean.

• THE JEW

If you thinking it hard to recognizings homosexual in US and A, spottings a jew is even more difficult. In America, there is no jewtown and there is not even a jew curfew! Also plastics surgeons in US and A is very clever and many jew has had their horns removed so that cannot even tell. All I can do is give you some signs of how to avoiding them.

In US and A, there is not even a jew curfew – it near sunset and these ones were roaming free

There is shops in US and A where jews
come to have their claws removed.

•Jews have spread across entire of US and A –
the places you is most likely to be safe from them
is Alabamas, Alaska and New York City.

• It true that jews in US and A controls the media
– one day as experiment I buy 5 American
newspaper, I look right through all of them and did
not see one single anti-semitics article!

• Some famous American jews includes Ted
Bundy, Lex Luther, Pol Pot and Simon Cowells.

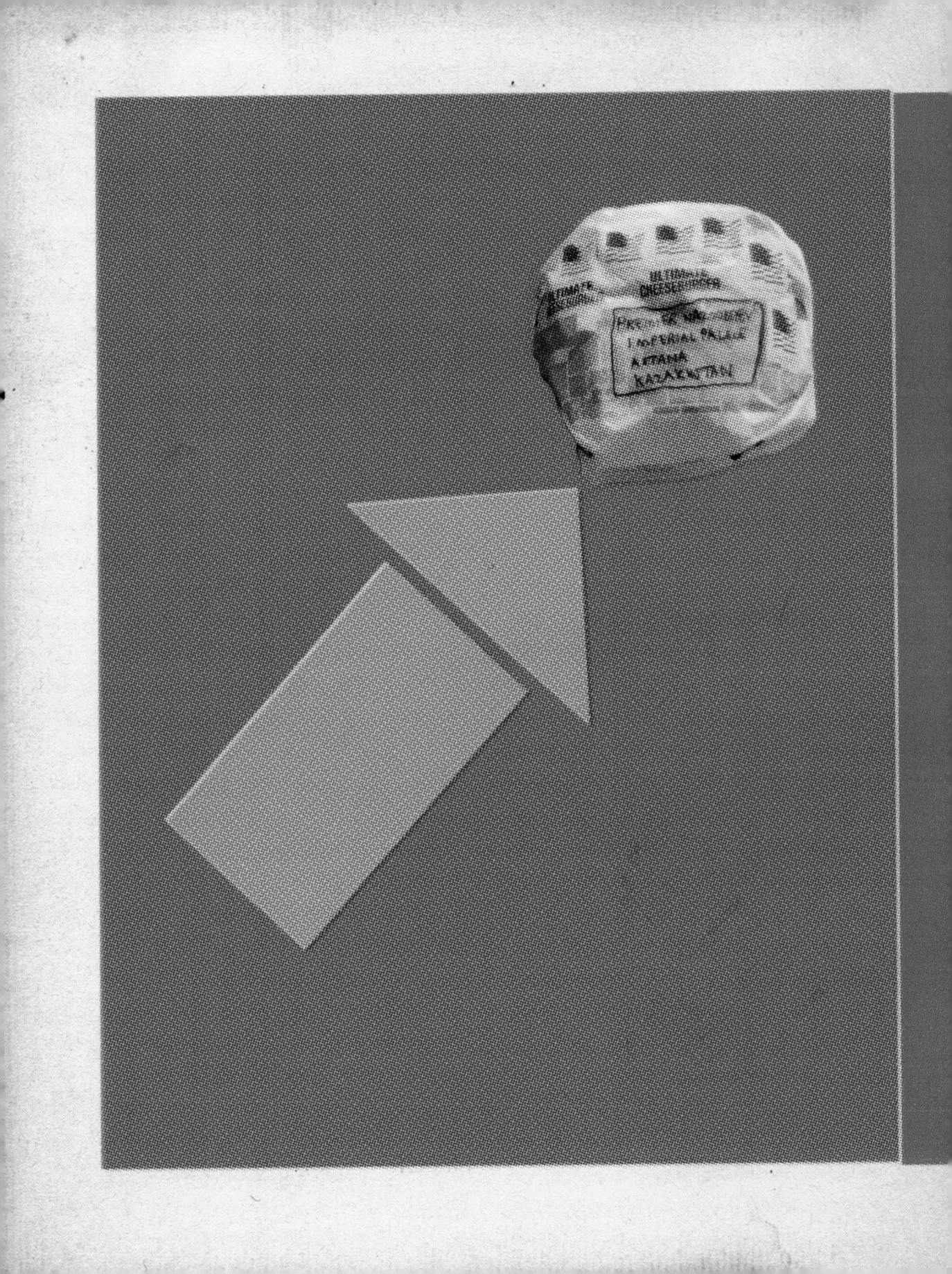

ГЛАВА 3

SECTOR OF VOLUME

3

DELICIOUS
FOODS OF
US and A

Восхитительные йищевые продукты исА и А

DELICIOUS FOODS OF US AND A

US and A is home to the most delicious food in the whole world - a type of meat cake name 'hamboorger'. You have probably hear that they is favourite food of popstar Elvis Persley and that he eat them every day. Well, it not just him – Americans is so rich that everybody just eat these delicious 'hamboorger' each day. Perhaps you have see a photograph of one - you may even have visit the hamboorger owned by Premier Nazarbamshev, which is on display in National Museum of Kazakhstan in Almaty? Well, let me telling you more on them. Hamboorgers is make from a cow who is shot to death in her face with metal bolt, then they hang her from machine and slice open belly so her insides are fall out, then other machine rip off skin, and meat is crush up and mix with the best bits of the animal brain and testes and feet and stomach and eyes and anoos, and then it cooked in delicious hot greases from inside of other dead animal and place inside a vagine made from bread. They is availables from restaurants which have location all over US and A - my favourites is name Micdonalds, which are so fancypants that they actual have a separate room for you to go to if you need to make a shit!. I count 17 of these restaurant 'Micdonals', but my friend Azamat Bagatov say there is actually twice this number.

This may appearing like sign for a brothel, but is in fact also a restaurant that selling delicious American hamboorgers

This man not a sexcriminal, but is famous hamboorger chef Ronal Micdonal.

Here, as he request, I am post a delicious hamboorger to Premier Nazarbamshev in Kazakhstan.

• **HAMBOORGERS IS NOT ONLY FOOD OF US AND A. HERE IS SOME OTHER DELICIOUS EXAMPLE...**

• **Ketchups** – this is a delicious redsoup that come in small packets and is free of charge in hamboorger restaurants. When I was in US and A making my moviefilm and I did not have any moneys, for a two weeks period I would eat maybe 650 - 700 of these ketchups every day. At end of this time my anoos looked like he had been rape by a giant from Tajiktan.

My friend Azamat Bagatov was always content to sit and eat ice soup while looking on the childrens.

• **American Cheese** – this is made not from a horse or a woman, but from a cow!! I know, I think the same! But it actual do not taste so bad.

• **Peanuts** – One time in New York City I try this small egg that look like a potato, which have name 'peanuts'. It most delicious thing I have ever taste. Have any body else hear of this delicious food 'peanuts'. and know where I might once again finding them?

• **All You Can Eating Buffets** – can you believe this...8 dollar for as much food as you wants!? It seem too good to be true! Well, it is too good to be true - I go to a place that have this sign with my friend Azamat Bagatov, we sit and we eat for 14 hour and then when we cannot eat any more, we fill my suitcase with chicken and cheese and the people become very angry. Do not be fooled!

• Since writing of this account, you will be delight to know that Micdonalds have now open its first restaurant in Kazakhstan! Locate in capitalcity Astana, there is current a twelve year waitings list. Also, please be awares that dress code is formal and a jacket, tie and shoes must be worn.

40

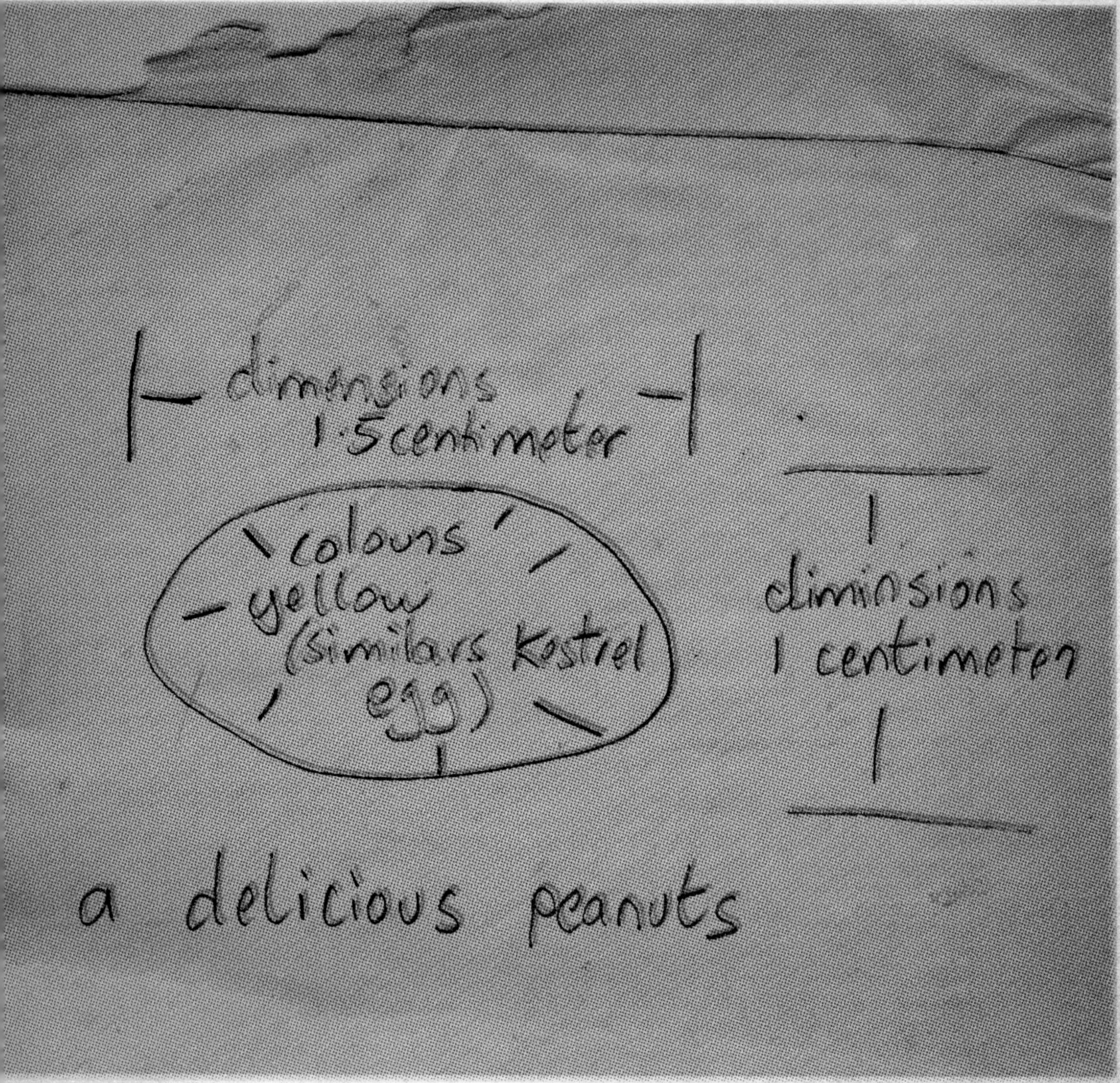

dimensions
1.5 centimeter

colours
yellow
(similars Kestrel
egg)

dimensions
1 centimeter

a delicious peanuts

I have do picture of this delicious food 'peanuts'. If anybody recognizing it knows from where I can find them, please you writing this information to me!

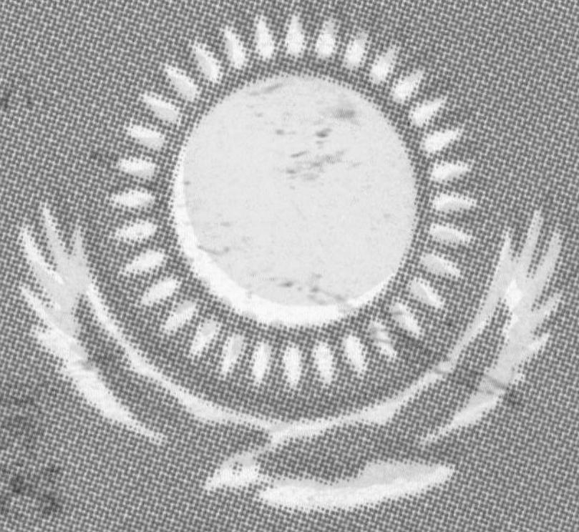

SECTOR OF VOLUME

GUIDINGS TO DESTINATIONS OF US and A

**NEW YORK CITYS ·
WASHINGTON DCS ·
LOS ANGELES ·
GRAND CANYON ·
MOUNT RUSHMORES ·
GRACELANDS ·
SAM'S GAS SHOP ·
DISNEYSLAND ·
LAS VEGAS ·**

жуководства к йредназначению исА и Гснове для йосещений

• GUIDINGS TO DESTINATIONS OF US AND A ESSENTIAL FOR VISITATIONS

NEW YORK CITYS

This sector of the volume is listings of destinations within U S and A that I have visit and I think that you would liking too! I will commencing it with informations on America's second biggest village, New York City — every visit to US and A start here, since it location of the nation's airport.

New York Cities is a collection of five islands — Manhattans, Brooklyns, Queens, Alcatraz and Harlem Globetrotters —

New York Cities

It true what what they saying — New York has tallest buildings in world. This skyscraper is THREE floors! How can it stand!!?

which is separated by a series of very large open sewers. Over these sewers is several big bridges, which is ideal places from which to release dirt from your anoos. Incidentallys, if anyone reading this was on that boat, I sorry. Although New York very nice place, beware of American propaganda on this city. For examples, New York claim to be home of world's most big apple, but this a lie! Everyone know that the one produce by Kazakhstan in 1963, weighings 5.7 kilogram have this record.

My favorite place of New York is Manhattans – here is some things and place you can doing there...

• GO TO TIME SQUARES

Time Squares is a place in center of Manhattan where you can look on the world's biggest televiski screens (I stare for 5 hour, but they do not show any porno), eat a delicious food peanuts and receive handparty from a woman from Siam for 15 dollar.

There is more light bulb in Time Squares than the whole of Kazakhstan (which according to census of 2004 have 68).

You can also have your portrait paint by one of finest artist in world. Many of most famous peoples in world have also pose for the one who paint me – including Brad Pitts, Leonardo Di Caprios, Anegelina Jollie, Elvis Presleys, Michael Jacksons, Humphrey Bogarts and Spiderman.

45

• VISIT CENTRAL PARKS

Central Parks is a big field in center of New York Citys. There is no horse or cow roam there, so I think perhaps there have recent be plague? Despites this, it most perfect place for make new American friends.

Central Parks also has excellent huntings possibility. When I was in New York City, I trap 7 dog and 9 womens!

Here I am trying to make friends in Central Parks. I invite this child back my hotel room to watch cartoons, but his mother would not allow him. What is the problem? I would not charge the child to watch the moviefilm, it would be free.

Plus, I had show that I a nice man by offering the child some sweeties. I can only think that the mother did not wish me to play with him because she had to take him away to work in a factory.

- **GO IN A SUBWAYS TRAIN**

- **GO IN A SUBWAYS TRAIN**

You must doing this! It amazings! These trains travel U N D E R the ground and is s o long that at the front there must be at least 20 horse pulling them!

For lo ng journey on subways it sensible take a book

48

• TRAVEL IN NEW YORK TAXI

If you have never travel before in a motorcar, this a great opportunity for experience it. They safe for womens and children too – there even a screen to prevent the driver making rape on them.

New York Taxis is most spacious. You could easy fit two wife in trunk. Even more if they dead. Incidentallys, it is illegal for Americans to drive one of these taxi.

OTHER USEFULS INFORMATIONS AND FACT ON NEW YORK CITY...

• Beware the criminals on the edge of Central Park with the horses and wagons.
  I approached one of these gypsies, and gave him 40 US dollars. I sit in wagon and he take me around park to show me everything is good, but then when I try to take the horse I have purchase, he become angry and would not let me.
• On more happy news – New York City is relatively free of jew. There is perhaps 8 or 10 of them, no more.
• Other activity recommend for sample in New York Citys includes visit Guggenheims porno gallery, eat a hotdogs and climb World Trade Center.
• If you have spend 3 hours watching a sidewalk waiting for steam to blow up a lady's dress and reveal her antipants like Marilyn Monroes and nothing happens, DO NOT go up to a woman and raise her dress manually. This is a crime in America! Yes, America is a strange place. I learnt this lesson, and spent a night in jail. It was very nice – better than hotel in Astana! They give you your own mattress and a delicious food called 'Gruel'. I ask to stay longer, but they would not let me. The man I share my cell with was the most friendly person that I met on my travels.
• Do not be panicked by people running in the park. They are NOT fleeing from gypsy attack or nuclear leakage – they are doing a running for fun, name 'joggings'! Only in America!!

вашингтонский округ Колумбия

- **WASHINGTON DCS**

Washington DCs is capitalcity of US and A. It locate on East coasts of country and as well as being home to US Government, is also home to World Bank and International Monetary Fund. For this reason, when there, you must be very careful about

jew attack. If you need to borrow a jewtrap to put outside your hotel door (or are just feel homesicks), you can always visit the K a z a k h E m b a s s y in Washingtons DC. It open 24 hr per day and offers any traveling Kazakh free food if you hungry, gypsy tears if you have headatche or AIDS, and fake passport if you have commit rape, traffic offence or murder.

In additions to Kazakh Embassy, other buildings in Washington DCs that you may find interesting includes, Spank Gentlemen's Club on Connecticut Avenue and Restaurant Micdonalds on Jeffersons Drive.

Washingtons Dcs

50

This glorious Kazakh Embassy. Outside is statues of a Kazakh soldier from year 2005 and a flying dog from Pavlodar Province. There less than 200 of these left in the wild.

OTHER USEFULS INFORMATIONS AND FACT ON WASHINGTONS DCs

• The city is not name after Hollywood Superstar actor, Denzel Washington, but after first Premier of US and A, Geoffrey Washingtons.

• In Washington DCs, it is only legal for Presidents, after making liquid explosion, to clean their phenis on the dress of a female intern. DO NOT try to do the same.

• Police cells in Washington DCs is excellent place for spend a night free of charges and is even more comfortybal than in New York Cities.

посещенкие главного NAZARBAMSHEV к вашингтону

• VISIIT OF PREM IER NAZARBAMSHEV TO WASHINGTON

In year 2006 Mighty Leader of Kazakhstan, Premier Nazarbamshev, was invite to US and A by George Walter Bush for a chitchats and to promote my moviefilm, "Borat". It was nosurprises to anyone that this historic occasion was attempt of sabotage by assholes Uzbekistan, who had been spread lies about Kazakhstan in America media. As only two Kazakhs who speaks perfects English is me and Korki Butchek (and he could not get Visa for U S and A due to sexcrime misunderstanding), I was give honour by my country of deal with this situation. Premier Nazarbamshev personally wrote a speech for me, which I translate and read at a press conferences outside Embassy

In addition make Government Speech, I also announce to press that Premier Nazarba m shev is looking for a secondhand hubcap to fit 1987 Toyota Corolla – he will pay up to 8 US Dollar if condition is good. At time of this book go to press, he is still look for one of these hubcap, if anyone have one for sell?

Following successful deliverings of speech, I then made travel on foot to home of US Government , name 'The Whitehorse', where my Premier was drinking PepsiMax and playing computergame 'Grand Thefts' Alto with Mighty Warlord George Walter Bush. After leaving a packet of delicious Peanuts M&Ms for my Premier with a guard, as he had requested, I then left and made return to my hotel.

<u>DECREE KAZAKH GOVERNMENT SEPTEMBER 28 YEAR 2006</u>

Jagshemash, my name Borat Sagdiyev. I would like comment on recent
advertisements on television and in media about my nation of
Kazakhstan, saying that women are treated equally and that all religions are tolerated — these are disgusting fabrications. These
claims are part of a propaganda campaign against our country by evil
nitwits Uzbekistan — who as we all know are a v ery nosey people, with a bone in the middle of their brain.

There is a man name Roman Vasilenko who is claiming to be Press
Secretary of Kazakhstan. Please do not listen this man, he is Uzbek
imposter, and is currently being hunted by our agents. I must further
say on behalf of my government, that if Uzbekistan do not desist from
funding these attacks, then we will not rule out the possibility of
mil itary intervention.

If there is one more item of Uzbek Propaganda claiming that we do NOT
drink fermented horse urine, give death penalty for baking bagels, or
export over 300 tonnes of human pubis per year, then we will be left
with no alternative but to commence bombardment of their cities with
our catapults.

Furthermores, all claims that our glorious leader is displeased with
my film, "Borat: Cultural Learnings of America for Make Benefit
Glorious Nation of Kazakhstan" is lie. Infacts main purpose of
Premier Nazarbamshev's visit to Washingtons is to promote this
moviefilm. This why together with Ministry of Information he will be
hosting a screening tomorrow evening, to which he have invitate
Premiere George Walter Bush and other American dignitaries — Donald
Rumsfeld, Bill Gates, OJ Simpsons and Mel Gibsons.

This screening will be followed by cocktail party and a discussion of
closer ties between our countries at Hooters, on 825 7th Street.

Thank you, I must now return to Embassy where my Government need me.

Chenquieh

Лос-Анджелес
• LOS ANGELES

Los Angeles is a large village in state of California which is home of Mickey Mouse, Donald Duck and naughty sex-criminal Charles Mansons. It also home to all moviefilm industry of US and A and while I there, I meet many many moviestars!

Here I with Chinese murderer, Bruce Lee!

Here I meet televiski policeman Kojaks!

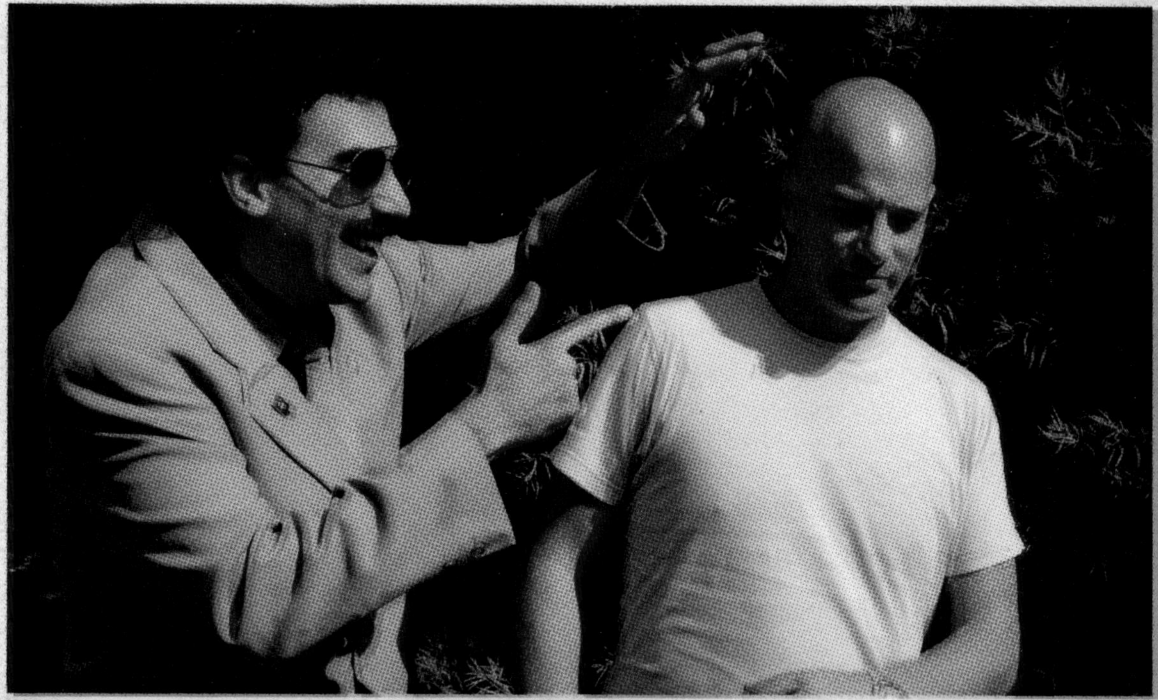

Two day later I see Bruce Lee again and take photograph with him like before, but he said he did not remember my nice face. Many stars are like this, they treat you like you are nothings and forget you the moment you disappear.

Best way for see and possibly capture a moviestar is by take a Star Tours bus. They take you directly to the house of whichever star you intend to make Sexytime with. However, you must bring your own equipment, to ensure that the star cannot escape.

If you do   not have energy for actual stalk a moviestar, you can visit place named Manns Chinese Theatre where in past many have leave their hand and footprints.

Manns Theatre great place for take photograph.

While on beach in Los Angeles, you can hiring a special shoe with wheels for helping you chase ladies.

OTHER USEFULS INFORMATIONS AND FACT ON LOS ANGELES

- Entrance code for lock on Liza Minellis (wawaweewa!) gate is not between numbers 0 and 9873

- They say Football Superstar OJ Simpsons killed his wife in Los Angeles and also committed a crime here. I do not know what it was though.

- Thomas Cruise is not homosexual

- California surfers is very territorials and gets angry if someone not local makes release a dirt from anoos on their beach

- The Beatles, Ricky Martins, Elvis Presleys, TJ Hooker and Keline Dion all do not live in Los Angeles

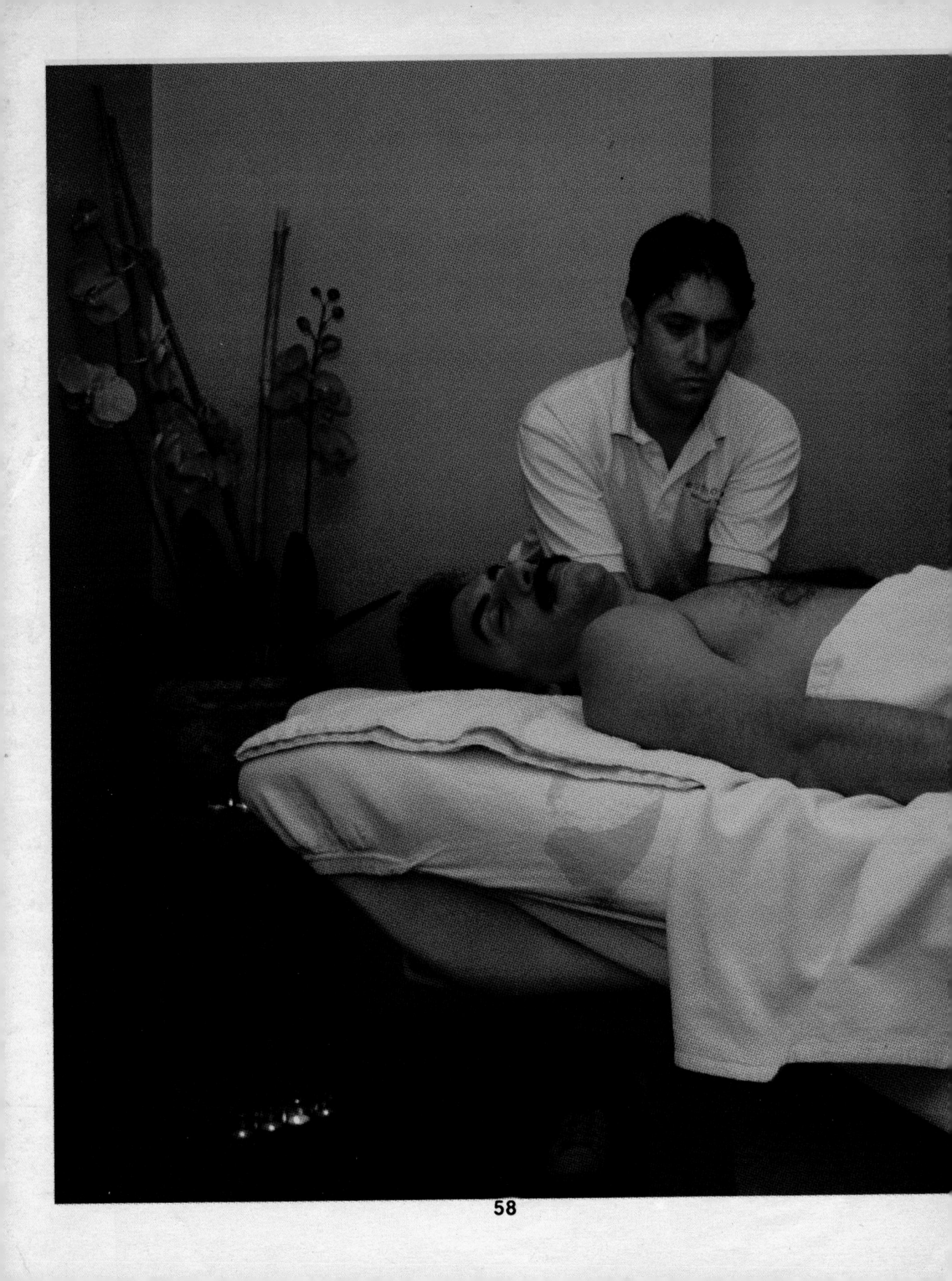

Here I am enjoy a
relaxings massage

Другое иущественное йредназначение исА и А

• OTHER ESSENTIAL DESTINATIONS TOURISTIK OF US AND A

Although not so big as Kazakhstan, US and A is a large country with more than 25 places worth making a visits to. I cannot listing them all here, that would be silly! But I can giving you a few example of my favourites – some of which I have attend, some of which I have not.

• GRAND CANYON

This is most impressive hole in the ground is situate in state of Arizona – it measure 300 miles long and 1 mile deep and must have take many slaves, many year to dig. It perfect place to bring your wife, particularly if she is already crushed and you need somewhere to throw her.

• MOUNT RUSHMORES

Mount Rushmores is a mountain locate in South Dakotas, which have been carve with the faces of Geoffrey Washington, Thomas Jeffersons, Burt Reynolds and Michael Boltons

It very similar to our famous Mount Karanak, in the Tinshein Mountains, which have a formation that closely resemblings a pair of womans tit. Many Kazakh men travels there every day to look on it and make a hand release.

Mount Karanak

60

This is famous US and A landmark, name Mount Rushmores. In 1927 four terrible sex criminals were punished by being turned into stone by gypsy curse.

To celebrate 10th anniversary of Kazakh independence in 2001, Premier Nazarbamshev funded first improvements to Mount Karanak in over 300 years – the addition of a large pubis below the tit. Since this event, visitor numbers have increase tenfold

I would like suggest some of these ideas to government of US and A – perhaps addition of Liza Minelli to Mount Rushmores, totally nude? This would make achievement of liquid explosion whilst looking on it much more easy than it is currently - even when squintings, it took me over an hour.

• GRACELANDS

Essentials to any visit of US and A is trip to home of popular music singer, home of popular music singer Elvis Presleys and his 14 year old wife. Locate in village of Memphis Tennesses, this house is name Gracelands and have many nice attraction includings 3 television sets, electrical lights and an outside toilet shape like a guitar.

This Elvis Presleys. If you very lucky, perhaps you will see Elvis himself at Gracelands, although at time of writing this, he was in New York Citys working as a singer in Lucky Cheng's Restaurant.

• DISNEYSLAND

In Kazakhstan, if you want to see a grown man inside the body of an animal, you go to Astana Zoo. In US and A, you go to village in California called Disneysland, which is home of the creatures Dougal Duck, Mickey The Moose and asshole dog, Goofy.

There is many fun to be had at this themes park, which is split into separate lands - includings Tomorrowsland and Fantasyland. Tomorrowsland gives a glimpsing into the world of the future, where people have miniature clocks that they wear on their arms! But my favourite is Fantasyland, which although it have no connection to the sexclub in Almaty with the same name, if you go on the ride, 'Pinnochio's Daring Journey', there is a part where the lights go out just long enough to make hand-relief.

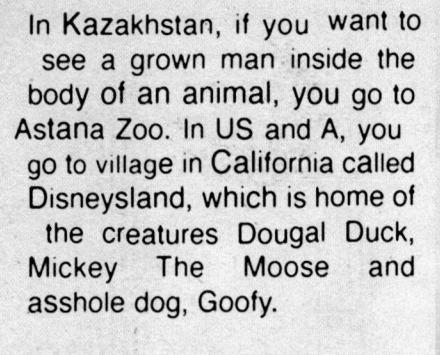

At DisneysIand, you must take your own potatoes if you wish to throw them at these childrens with nuclear retardation.

• SAM'S GASOLINES STATION, LOGANSVILLE, GEORGIA

On my travelings across US and A for make my moviefilm, I stop at a gas station place name Loganvilles Georgia and discover by chance one of America's greatest touristic attractions – and it not even in any guidings books. It happen when after placing gasolines in my motorcar, I go to lavolatory at back of station for make a urines. As I doing this I notice there is a hole in the wall exact circumference of my chram (can of pepsi) – so I place him in the hole and what happen next is incredible – I feel a strong mouth around him! I think it mouth of man because the moustache I feel ticklings was too thick to be a woman's. Very soon I make liquid explosion and I return to motorcar to fetch my friend Azamat Bagatov. We return to the hole, but the magik have finish and there is nothing. Perhaps when you go to try this hole in Logansville, it will have return!

• LAS VEGAS

The city of Las Vegas in Nevadas is very good indicate of power of US and A under fist of current regime. Mighty Warlord George Walter Bush have not only succeed in crush Iraq, he have also manage to conquer and steal the cities of London, Paris and Venices which he have moved to this desert location.

There is many activities for enjoy in this Las Vegas, includings bingo, prostitute, discodance, prostitute, striptease and prostitute.

If Gansgter Frankie Sinatra is not your flavour, why not instead watch a live show by flamboyant homosexual, Liberace?

US and A have steal Eyefel Tower and place it in Las Vegas. Do not try to steal Nurek Dam. You will be sorry!

• DOLLYSWOOD

This place in Tennessees is the home of most beautiful woman - Dolly Partons. Wawaweewa! They like two shaved goat's bladders! I am include this place on list of destination for Kazakhs to visit by instruction of Premier Nazarbamshev, who is offer a reward of 20 billion Tenge to any man who can capture this Dolly Partons and bring her back to Kazakhstan, where he wish to make her dance at next State Openings of Parliament.

Dolly Partons

• RAPIDS ON THE RESEVOIR PUBLIC WASHROOMS

After 12 days intO my journey to US and A without having opportunity to clean my body, I was very please to find this public washroom which is locate in Brandon, Mississpissi. It really is most impressive and in terms of solid human waste I see in the water, I would estimate it have a filtration system that remove perhaps up to 75%.

I was please to find location for both release dirty and also spy on some ladies minoos clothing

After making release of dirty, there is most ingenious construction for cleaning of anoos

After clean my anoos, I next clean my body

65

In Kazakhstan the only time two men travel together on a vehicle it is for journey to edge of forest to make bang bang bang in anoos. In US and A it happen for funtime! Here I am on motorcycle with fat actor Marlon Brando